—FIT FOR—
A _P_RINCESS
—100—
PRIZEWINNING RECIPES
IN AID OF CHILD 2000

FIT FOR A PRINCESS

100
PRIZEWINNING RECIPES
IN AID OF CHILD 2000

Foreword by
HRH The Princess of Wales

Hodder & Stoughton

LONDON SYDNEY AUCKLAND TORONTO

British Library Cataloguing in Publication Data
Fit for a princess.
  1. Diana. Princess of Wales. 2. Cookery
I. Prima (London)
641

  ISBN 0-340-53161-4

Published by Hodder and Stoughton,
a division of Hodder and Stoughton Ltd,
Mill Road, Dunton Green, Sevenoaks, Kent TN13 2YA
Editorial Office: 47 Bedford Square, London WC1B 3DP

Photoset by Rowland Phototypesetting (London) Ltd
Printed in Great Britain by Butler and Tanner Ltd, Frome and London

Photography of HRH The Princess of Wales by Terence Donovan

Contents

Foreword by HRH The Princess
of Wales   7

Introduction   9

Starters   11

Vegetarian Dishes   31

Main Courses   47

Cakes and Puddings   95

Index   141

Acknowledgments   144

KENSINGTON PALACE

Proceeds from this book will help Child 2000 in its commitment to the elimination of unnecessary and preventable suffering by immunising children against the major childhood diseases and the eradication of these tragic viruses by the year 2000.

As Patron of Child 2000 (The National Council for Child Health) I send my very best wishes to those involved in this vital work and my thanks to all who give it their support.

January, 1991

Diana

Introduction

While it is true to say that every cookery book you see in print is a team effort, the team working on this particular book was well over one hundred strong!

This exciting collection of recipes created by the readers of *Prima* magazine is the result of a very special competition. *Prima* readers were asked to create recipes that they felt were truly Fit for a Princess and by so doing support a charity that really is very important. All the royalties from this book will benefit CHILD 2000, the National Council for Child Health, and happily for us, their Patron, The Princess of Wales, has kindly written a Foreword and accepted the very first copy of FIT FOR A PRINCESS on the behalf of this young but well-established charity.

Created in 1983 and originally known as the National Rubella Council, the charity was founded to increase the use of the rubella vaccination. Now it is newly relaunched as CHILD 2000, the National Council for Child Health, and has expanded to include a partnership of eleven of the UK's leading charities, together with the Department of Health and the Health Education Authority. This powerful group is determined to work towards a healthier Britain.

CHILD 2000 has a vital task: the reduction and elimination of all major childhood diseases in the United Kingdom by the year 2000. To achieve this CHILD 2000 needs to promote all the major vaccinations currently in mass circulation so that all children can have the protection they surely deserve. There are still many diseases causing death and tragic disability throughout society that can be prevented. Mumps, measles, rubella, diphtheria, whooping cough, tetanus, polio and others still represent a threat. With the help of the public, CHILD 2000 will reduce and even extinguish this threat so that these diseases can cause no more death, no more blindness, deafness, brain damage and other permanent disabilities.

CHILD 2000's single daunting objective is to meet the World Health Organisation's target, ensuring that at least ninety-five per cent of all our children and young adults are immunised against all these diseases by 1995. If this target is achieved, these diseases will no longer have the strength to wreak havoc throughout the nation and so much preventable suffering will cease. This can however only be achieved by partnership. A partnership between CHILD 2000 and the people of this country. By purchasing this wonderful collection of creative cooking you will be helping CHILD 2000 in its vital work.

Julia Lindley-French
Director, CHILD 2000

Sue James
Editor, *Prima*

Starters

Blushing Smoked Trout Mousse

Serves: 4–6
Prep: 20 mins
Cook: 2 mins

¼ pint/150 ml fish stock

3 tbsp/45 ml gelatine

¼ pint/150 ml rosé wine

4 oz/125 g prawns

12 oz/350 g smoked trout fillets

½ pint/300 ml soured cream

4 tbsp/60 ml lemon juice

pinch paprika

Sîan Cook from Cold Ash in Berkshire created this recipe for a romantic Valentine dinner three years ago and it's now her husband's favourite!

Lightly grease four ramekin dishes. Pour a little of the stock into a small bowl, sprinkle over 2 tbsp/30 ml gelatine, and place over a saucepan of simmering water. Stir gently until the gelatine has dissolved and the liquid is clear. Add the rest of the stock and the wine. Pour half of the liquid into the base of the ramekins and leave to set.

Once set, divide the prawns between each ramekin and pour on the remaining liquid and leave to set.

Mix together the smoked trout and soured cream. Dissolve the remaining gelatine in a little water and add to the trout mixture with the paprika and lemon juice. Spoon on to the ramekins and leave to set in the fridge for a few hours.

Loosen the mousses by running a knife around the edges and by dipping the ramekin bases in hot water for a couple of seconds. Turn out on to plates and decorate with salad leaves. Serve with brown bread and butter triangles.

Salmon Mousse

Serves: 6–8
Prep: 15 mins
Cook: 2 mins

3 oz/75 g small packet cream cheese

3 fl oz/75 ml mayonnaise

4 tsp/20 ml sachet of gelatine

7 oz/198 g can of red/ pink salmon

3 tomatoes, chopped

5 spring onions, chopped

Sally Ardagh from Lewes, East Sussex, has been making this recipe for years. 'It's impressive yet really easy to make and is always greeted with real enthusiasm.'

Place the cream cheese and mayonnaise into a liquidiser or food processor and beat until smooth. Meanwhile dissolve the gelatine in the drained salmon liquid, by standing a cup in a pan of hot water and sprinkling the gelatine over the liquid. Add the chopped tomatoes and onions to the cheese mixture and beat again until smooth. Finally, add the salmon and dissolved gelatine and beat again. Pour the mixture into a 1 pint/600 ml mould and chill until set, for approximately 2–3 hours.

Remove the mousse from the fridge a few minutes before it is required and allow it to reach room temperature as this makes it easier to remove from the mould. Turn out on to serving plate and decorate with sliced cucumbers, lettuce or watercress. Serve with toast or crusty bread.

Smooth Chicken Paté

Serves: 4–6
Prep: 10 mins
Cook: 10–15 mins

8 oz/225 g chicken livers

8 oz/225 g butter

2 cloves garlic, crushed

1 tsp/5 ml mixed herbs

juice of one orange

2 tbsp/30 ml brandy or sherry

salt and pepper to taste

bayleaves and peppercorns

Once you've tasted this fast and easy-to-make chicken paté you'll never bother to buy the ready made kind again! Mrs H. E. Cobb of Swindon created the clever recipe.

Place 4 oz/125 g butter into a saucepan, add the remaining ingredients and bring to the boil. Simmer for 20–30 minutes. Allow to cool slightly and blend in food processor or liquidiser until smooth. Put into a ramekin dish and allow to cool.

Melt the remaining butter and allow to cool slightly. Pour the mixture through a fine sieve lined with kitchen paper and spoon the clarified butter over the cooled paté. Decorate with bayleaf and peppercorns and leave to set. Serve with triangles of toasted brown bread.

Salmon Mousse Ring, Savoury Artichoke Spread with Melba Toast, Blushing Smoked Trout and Smooth Chicken Paté

Savoury Artichoke Spread

Serves: 4
Prep: 8 mins
Cook: 15–20 mins

15 oz/425 g can artichoke hearts

3 oz/75 g Parmesan cheese, grated

7 tbsp/105 ml mayonnaise

1 large clove garlic, finely chopped

salt and black pepper

Try making this tangy spread in individual ramekin dishes and serve it as an elegant starter with slithers of Melba toast. Created by Betty Halls from Kessingland in Suffolk.

Preheat the oven to Gas Mark 4/350F/180C. Drain the artichoke hearts and grate the cheese.

In a mixing bowl combine the artichokes, cheese, mayonnaise and garlic. Add salt and pepper to taste. Spoon the mixture into a small greased ovenproof dish and bake for 15–20 minutes until bubbling and browned. Serve hot with toast as a starter or a savoury snack.

Garlic and Vermouth Mushrooms

Serves: 2–4
Prep: 20 mins
Cook: 15 mins

This most more-ish starter is one you'll make again and again. Serve it in small individual dishes with crusty rolls to mop up the juices. Devised by Mrs Teresa Gillam from Bridgwater in Somerset.

1 lb/450 g button mushrooms

2 oz/50 g butter

6 cloves garlic, crushed

salt and black pepper

¼ pint/150 ml martini or vermouth

1 tsp/5 ml cornflour

4 tbsp/60 ml single cream

parsley or chives to garnish

Wash and dry the mushrooms and melt the butter in a large saucepan. Add the mushrooms, garlic, salt and black pepper and vermouth and put the lid on the pan. Simmer over a medium heat for 10–15 minutes, stirring occasionally until the mushrooms are cooked. Mix the cornflour with a small amount of water to make a paste and pour on to the mushrooms, stirring continuously. Leave to cool slightly then stir in the cream. Serve sprinkled with a little parsley.

Tip: If the mushrooms are too large cut them into quarters.

Fresh Melon with Stem Ginger and Yoghurt Sauce, Mock Lobster Soufflé, Garlic and Vermouth Mushrooms and Prawn and Brie Strudels with Yoghurt Dip

Fresh Melon with Stem Ginger and Yoghurt

Serves: 4
Prep: 10–15 mins
Cook: No cook

1 medium sized melon, seeds removed

4 oz/125 g jar stem ginger, finely chopped

½ pint/300 ml thick natural yoghurt

mint, to garnish

A cool and fruity starter with a creamy sauce that has a hidden surprise – spicy pieces of stem ginger. From Janet Fothergill of Luton in Bedfordshire.

Slice melon into 4 or 6 slices. To make the sauce, chop the stem ginger into very small pieces and place in a basin with the yoghurt and juice from the ginger. Transfer to a serving jug and serve with the melon. Garnish with a sprig of mint.

Tip: This sauce is just as delicious served with other fresh fruit such as pineapple, kiwifruit or mango.

Prawn and Brie Strudels

Serves: 4–6
Prep: 15–20 mins
Cook: 15 mins

These delicious little filo parcels of prawns and melted Brie make elegant mouthfuls and super starters. Kate Fryer of Tunbridge Wells in Kent also suggests you try other fillings like curried chicken, smoked trout or asparagus and crispy bacon.

1 oz/25 g butter, melted

4 sheets filo pastry

6 oz/175 g prawns, chopped

2 oz/50 g Brie, chopped

grated rind of one lemon

3 oz/75 g cucumber, grated

5 oz/141 g carton natural yoghurt

3 tbsp/45 ml single cream

salt and pepper to taste

cherry tomatoes, to garnish

Preheat the oven to Gas Mark 6/400F/200C. Brush 2 sheets of pastry with the melted butter and place one on top of the other. Cut the sheets in half to make two rectangles and repeat with the remaining pastry.

Spoon a quarter of the prawn mixture 1 in/2.5 cm along the pastry edge. Top with the Brie and sprinkle with the lemon rind. Season with salt and pepper. Brush the edges with butter. Fold in the edges and roll up with the filling to form a strudel. Place seam side down on a baking sheet and brush with butter. Repeat with the remaining pastry. Bake in oven for fifteen minutes until golden brown.

In a bowl mix together the cucumber, yoghurt and cream and season to taste. Serve with the prawn strudels, garnished with cherry tomatoes.

Mock Lobster Soufflé

Serves: 4–6
Prep: 10 mins
Cook: 20 mins

Serve something sophisticated at your next dinner party. This magical soufflé looks spectacular and yet it's pretty inexpensive to make. Top marks to Mrs E. Ritchie of Haddington, East Lothian.

3 eggs

8 oz/225 g white fish

4 oz/125 g lobster or crab

3 tbsp/45 ml single cream

1 tbsp/15 ml flour

1 tbsp/15 ml anchovy sauce

2 tsp/10 ml tomato purée

1 tsp/5 ml curry powder

1 tbsp/15 ml sherry

salt and pepper to taste

Grease a 2 pint/1.2 litre soufflé dish or 4–6 individual ramekins.

Separate the eggs and place the egg yolks with the remaining ingredients into a liquidiser or food processor and mix until smooth.

Whisk the egg whites until stiff and carefully and evenly fold into fish mixture with a large metal spoon. Spoon into prepared dish and bake in the oven for 20 minutes. Serve immediately.

Leek and Roquefort Soup

Serves: 4
Prep: 10 mins
Cook: 15 mins

A really glamorous soup with a sophisticated flavour created by Nicola Simpson, a thirteen-year-old schoolgirl from Bromley High School in Kent, is just one of the very original recipes she entered.

2 large leeks

1 large potato

1 pint/600 ml vegetable stock

3 oz/75 g Roquefort cheese, cubed

Wash and roughly chop the leeks and potato and simmer the vegetables in the stock for 15 minutes. Place vegetables, stock and Roquefort in a liquidiser and blend into a purée. Season to taste. Delicious served with soft white rolls, placed in a hot oven for 2 minutes before serving.

Tip: Stilton can also be used. Why not use up any remains from the cheeseboard?

Carrot and Coriander Seed Soup

Serves: 6
Prep: 30 mins
Cook: 30 mins

1 oz/25 g butter

1 tbsp/15 ml oil

2 tsp/10 ml coriander seeds

1 tsp/5 ml ground coriander

1½ lb/700 g carrots, peeled and roughly chopped

1½ pints/900 ml vegetable stock

fresh coriander, to garnish

For sheer good looks and an exotic flavour this golden soup just can't be beaten. A fast and easy to make recipe from Anna Ind of London.

Heat the butter and oil in a pan. Add the coriander seeds and ground coriander and fry until seeds darken. Add the carrots and stir-fry for another few minutes before adding the vegetable stock. Bring to the boil and simmer until carrots are tender. Remove from heat and liquidise until smooth. Re-heat and serve garnished with chopped coriander leaves and slices of brown bread.

Tip: Homemade vegetable stock is much the best to use. However, for speed and just as good flavour, look out for ready-made vegetable stock in large supermarkets.

Mrs M's Mussel Soup

Serves: 4
Prep: 20 mins
Cook: 20 mins

1 lb/450 g mussels

2 oz/50 g butter

1 small onion, chopped

1 clove garlic, crushed

½ pint/300 ml white wine

2 potatoes, diced

1 carrot, grated

1 shallot, chopped

1 tomato, skinned

1 tbsp/15 ml parsley, chopped

1 tsp/5 ml celery salt

¼ pint/150 ml single or low-fat cream

A main course soup that's delicious served with lots of crusty bread to mop up the very last drop! A fabulous recipe from Anne Mathewson of Darley, North Yorkshire.

To prepare for cooking pull off the beard from each mussel and scrub shells clean.

In a large saucepan melt half the butter and sauté the onion and garlic until soft. Add the mussels and wine and cover and cook for about 7–10 minutes, until the shells open. Discard any unopened shells.

Melt the remaining butter in a large pan and sauté the potatoes, carrots, shallots and tomato for 5 minutes. Add the mussels and liquid and cook for a further 10 minutes. Remove from the heat and add the cream. Stir well, and serve with a salad and crusty bread for a lovely lunch.

Tip: Mussels are generally available when there is an 'r' in the month.

If you've extra time, soak the mussels in salty water for one hour before cooking to remove any grit from inside shells.

Mushroom Bisque

Serves: 4
Prep: 5 mins
Cook: 40 mins

2 oz/50 g butter

2 cloves garlic, crushed

8 oz/225 g mushrooms, chopped

2 tbsp/30 ml brandy

3 fl oz/75 ml dry white wine

½ pint stock/300 ml chicken stock

½ pint/10 fl oz/284 ml carton single cream

parsley, chopped to garnish

The ultimate dinner party soup from Sue Butcher of Lower Compton, Plymouth. Rich with white wine, cream and brandy it's ideal for those really special occasions.

Melt the butter in a large pan and add the garlic and mushrooms and sauté on a low heat for about 10 minutes. Add 1 tbsp/15 ml of the brandy, warm the remainder in a ladle then light with a match and pour over the mushrooms and garlic, stirring all the time. Increase the heat and pour in the wine and stock and allow to simmer gently for 30 minutes. Pour into a liquidiser or food processor and blend until smooth. Return to the pan and stir in half the cream and reheat gently. Serve in bowls with a swirl of cream and sprinkle with fresh parsley.

Over the page, left: Carrot and Coriander Soup, Leek and Roquefort Soup and Mrs M's Mussel Soup. Right: Mushroom Bisque, Cold Chive and Potato Soup with Cheese, Petit Pois and Courgette Soup and Spinach and Cheese Soup

Cold Chive and Potato Soup with Cheese

Serves: 4–6
Prep: 10 mins
Cook: 35 mins

Helen Frost of Cambridge transforms the flavour of her favourite chilled potato soup simply by using a different cheese or herb.

1 oz/25 g butter

1 medium onion

2 pints/1.2 litres chicken stock

14 oz/400 g potatoes

4 oz/125 g Stilton cheese, Cheddar or Brie

salt and pepper

1 tbsp/15 ml chives, chopped

1 tbsp/15 ml parsley, chopped

¼ pint/150 ml single cream

Peel and slice the potatoes and finely chop the onion. Melt the butter in a large pan and add the onion. Sauté until soft then add the chicken stock and potatoes and season to taste. Simmer together for 30 minutes. Liquidise the mixture with 3 oz/ 75 g cheese until smooth then mix in chives and parsley. Chill, then add cream and stir well. Serve cold with a sprinkling of remaining cheese and snipped chives.

Petits Pois and Courgette Soup

Serves: 4
Prep: 5 mins
Cook: 12 mins

1 small onion

8 oz/225 g courgettes

1 tbsp/15 ml sunflower oil

1 clove garlic, finely chopped

1½ pints/900 ml chicken stock

8 oz/225 g petit pois

salt and pepper to taste

pinch ground cloves

4 tbsp/60 ml single or half-fat cream

Light and refreshing, this creamy soup by Mary Chapman of Norwich can be served chilled in summer or hot in winter, and uses either fresh or frozen tiny peas.

Finely chop the onion and slice the courgettes. Heat the oil in a pan and sauté the onion and garlic until soft. Add the stock, petit pois and courgettes. Bring to the boil, reduce the heat and simmer for 5–7 minutes. Add the salt, pepper and ground cloves. Pour into a liquidiser or food processor and blend until smooth. Return to the pan and bring to the boil. Season again if needed. Remove from the heat and stir in the cream. Serve immediately.

Tip: For speed use frozen sliced courgettes.

Spinach and Cheese Soup

Serves: 4
Prep: 15 mins
Cook: 30 mins

A thick, warming and flavoursome soup that's perfect for cold winter evenings. Mrs A. Andrews from Sheldon in Birmingham suggests you eat it as she does – in front of a roaring fire!

2 oz/50 g margarine

1 small onion, chopped

2 garlic cloves, crushed

2 oz/50 g flour

½ tsp/2.5 ml ground cumin

2 pints/1.2 litres chicken stock

1 lb/450 g spinach, fresh or frozen, finely chopped

8 oz/225 g mature Cheddar cheese, grated

salt and pepper

Melt the margarine in a saucepan and sauté the onion and garlic until soft. Mix in the flour and cumin and stir continuously for 2 minutes. Gradually add the hot stock, stirring all the time. Add the spinach and salt and pepper and simmer gently for about 15–20 minutes. Purée in a food processor or liquidise and return to saucepan.

Just before serving add the cheese and continue to cook until melted. Add more seasoning if desired and serve with crusty bread.

Vegetarian
Dishes

Crispy Cheese Pancakes with Courgette Sauce

Serves: 4–8
Prep: 30 mins
Cook: 20 mins

Beth Barker from Kendal, Cumbria, has created a pancake recipe with a difference. These delicious pancakes stuffed with three cheeses are coated in breadcrumbs and deep fried!

for pancakes:

4 oz/125 g plain flour

pinch salt

4 eggs

2 tbsp/30 ml oil

7 fl oz/200 ml milk

oil for deep frying

for filling:

2 tbsp/30 ml pine nuts

2 tbsp/30 ml olive oil

6 oz/175 g button mushrooms, finely chopped

6 oz/175 g Ricotta cheese

4 oz/125 g Mozzarella cheese, grated

2 tbsp/30 ml Parmesan cheese, grated

4 oz/125 g breadcrumbs

To make the pancakes, sift the flour and salt into a bowl and add the 4 eggs and oil. Beat until the mixture is smooth and gradually add milk to form a smooth batter.

To cook the pancakes heat a little oil in a small frying pan. Add 2–3 tbsp/30–45 ml of batter and swirl evenly around the pan. Cook over a medium heat until golden brown. Toss or turn the pancake and cook other side. Repeat with the remaining batter to make 8 pancakes. Reserve 2 tbsp/30 ml of the batter for sealing.

For the filling, put the pine nuts into a dry pan and shake over heat until golden, remove from pan. In another pan, heat the olive oil and sauté mushrooms until soft. Mix together with the pine nuts and three cheeses. Divide this filling between the pancakes and brush the edges of the pancakes with a little of the reserved batter. Fold each pancake in half. Brush the rounded edge of the folded pancake with rest of reserved batter then fold the pancake in half again, pressing edges to seal in the filling. Brush each pancake with lightly beaten egg then cover with breadcrumbs. Deep fry in hot oil for about 5 minutes until golden brown. Serve with courgette sauce.

Courgette sauce:

½ oz/15 g butter

4 shallots

6 oz/175 g courgettes, sliced

salt and pepper to taste

To make the sauce melt the butter in a saucepan and cook the shallots for 1 minute. Add the sliced courgette and cook for a further 2 minutes, stirring occasionally. Add ¼ pint/150 ml water and bring to the boil. Reduce heat and cook uncovered for 15 minutes. Cool slightly, then purée in a liquidiser or blender. Return to the saucepan, season with salt and pepper and stir and heat through. Serve poured over pancakes and accompanied with brown rice.

Savoury Parsnip Scones

Serves: 4
Prep: 15 mins plus
** 30 mins chilling**
Cook: 10 mins

1 lb/450 g parsnips

10 oz/275 g plain tofu

2 tbsp/30 ml fresh chives, chopped

salt and pepper

wholemeal flour for coating

2 tbsp/ 30 ml oil

Tofu is so versatile it can be used in sweet or savoury dishes. Barbara Marshall from Birmingham uses it in these mouthwatering scones.

Peel and cut the parsnips into small pieces. Simmer for 15–20 minutes until just tender. Cool slightly, then mash with a fork. Mash the tofu with a fork and mix thoroughly with the mashed parsnips. Season with salt and pepper and chopped chives.

Divide the mixture into 8 balls, flatten to make scone shapes and roll in flour. Chill in the fridge for 30 minutes.

Heat the oil in a frying pan and cook scones for 10 minutes on each side until golden brown. Serve hot with mixed salad and jacket potatoes for a main meal.

Vegetarian Stuffed Marrow

Serves: 4
Prep: 20 mins
Cook: 30–40 mins

1 small onion, chopped

4 oz/125 g dried apricots, chopped

2 oz/50 g butter, diced

6 oz/175 g/Bombay mix

6 oz/175 g sage and onion stuffing

6 oz/175 g apple stuffing

1 packet peanuts, salted

1 tsp/5 ml chilli powder

pinch paprika

1 large marrow

2 tbsp/30 ml oil, for basting

Mrs Ann Winter from Little Stoke, Bristol, first cooked this recipe for some vegetarian friends and they loved it. When marrows are out of season she uses courgettes or peppers.

Chop the onion and apricots and dice the butter. Place in a large mixing bowl with the remaining ingredients *except* the marrow. Add enough boiling water, as instructed on each packet of stuffing mixture plus a little extra to make mixture moist. Once cool, blend the ingredients together until evenly mixed.

Cut the top of the marrow and scrape the flesh from the inside very carefully, but leaving a small amount to keep marrow firm. Fill the marrow with the mixed stuffing and replace the top. Brush the marrow with the oil and place on a baking tray. Cover with foil and cook for 30–40 minutes. Remove from the oven and cut the marrow into 2 in/5 cm slices. By using a cake slice transfer the marrow neatly on to the plate, carefully keeping it from losing the stuffing. Serve with a green salad.

Exotic Tofu, Crispy Cheese Pancakes with Courgette Sauce, Vegetarian Stuffed Marrow, Savoury Parsnip Scones and Melon Salad

Exotic Tofu with Melon Salad

Serves: 4–6
Prep: 20 mins
Cook: 15 mins

2 shallots

piece of fresh ginger

2 oz/50 g butter

1 clove garlic, crushed

1 tsp/5 ml ground cumin

1 tsp/5 ml coriander

½ tsp/2.5 ml cinnamon

½ tsp/2.5 ml cloves

1 tsp/5 ml turmeric

½ tsp/2.5 ml chilli

2 oz/50 g ground almonds

2 tbs/30 ml cornflour

½ pint/300 ml natural yoghurt

8 oz/225 g firm tofu

for the salad:

1 avocado

1 lime

half a melon

6 Chinese leaves

Here is another exciting tofu recipe with an accompanying cool green 'fruit' salad. Created by Mrs M. A. Brown, Paulton near Bristol.

Finely chop the shallots and ginger. Heat the butter in a pan and fry the shallots, garlic and ginger until soft. Add the spices and ground almonds and cook for a further 2 minutes. Remove from the heat.

Mix the cornflour with 4 fl oz/100 ml water and stir into the spice mixture. Add the yoghurt and stir well. Return the pan to the heat and simmer stirring all the time until well blended.

Add cubed tofu and stir gently. Continue to simmer for 10 minutes, stir occasionally to prevent sticking. Serve with Basmati rice and garnish with red pepper cut into thin strips.

To prepare the salad, cut avocado in half and remove the stone and skin. Cut into neat slices. Cut lime in half and squeeze juice over avocado to prevent browning. Cut melon into cubes. Arrange the shredded Chinese leaves on a serving dish and place the avocado and melon on the Chinese leaves. Garnish with slices of lime.

Savoury Pizzas

Serves: 4
Prep: 20 mins
Cook: 35 mins
      plus 1½
      hours rising

Mrs C. Harris from Rainham in Kent freezes all her leftover cooked vegetables and uses them to make these easy and very tasty pizzas.

for the base:

12 oz/350 g cooked potatoes, mashed

1 lb/450 g strong white bread flour

1 packet quick easy blend dried yeast

½ tsp/2.5 ml salt

2 tsp/10 ml oil

¼ pint/150 ml tepid water

topping:

1 tbsp/15 ml oil

2 large onions, chopped

10 oz/275 g mixed frozen vegetables

2 tbsp/30 ml tomato purée

4 oz/125 g cheese, grated

Preheat the oven to Gas Mark 5/375F/190C. Grease 2 × 10 in baking trays.

Mix all the pizza base ingredients with the tepid water to form a smooth dough. Knead lightly on a floured surface for about 10 minutes. Divide into two and put on to the baking trays. Form into 2 × 8 in/20 cm rounds using your fingers to press into shape. Leave in a warm place for about 1½ hours to rise.

Prepare the topping by heating the oil in a frying pan and cook the onions until soft. Stir in the frozen or any leftover cooked vegetables. When the pizza base has risen, spread the tomato purée over the base leaving a ½ in/1 cm rim round the outside. Divide the fried onion and vegetables between the pizzas. Sprinkle on the cheese and cook for 20–25 minutes. Serve hot with salad.

Tip: Freeze the uncooked pizza-bases to use another time from frozen.

Tangy Vegetable Au Gratin

Serves: 6–8
Prep: 45 mins
Cook: 1 hour

This golden bubbly supper dish from Jean Ryan of Walderslade, Kent, is a real family favourite. Filling and economical too. Make it a great midweek standby.

2 potatoes

4 leeks

4 carrots

4 oz/125 g mushrooms

1 large onion

2 leaves red cabbage

4 tomatoes

1 tsp/5 ml curry powder

salt and pepper

¾ pint/450 ml cheese sauce

Preheat the oven to Gas Mark 4/350F/180C. Thinly slice the potatoes and tomatoes and slice thickly the remaining vegetables. Parboil the potatoes, leeks, carrots and onions and drain. Arrange half the potatoes on the base of a large oven proof dish. Layer the other vegetables. Season lightly. Top with remaining potato slices. Mix the curry powder into the cheese sauce and pour over the vegetables. Bake in oven for 40 minutes until brown and crispy. Serve with a winter salad.

From top, clockwise: Tangy Vegetable Gratin, Macaroni and Lentil Bake, Savoury Pizza and Cheesy Spirals

Macaroni and Lentil Bake

Serves: 4
Prep: 30 mins
Cook: 40 mins

Laura Leece of Chorley, Lancashire, created this recipe while she was at university. It's cheap, delicious and very nutritious, a perfect vegetarian main course.

1 onion

1 small green pepper

1 small yellow pepper

2 oz/50 g mushrooms

14 oz/396 g can tomatoes

6 oz/175 g split red lentils

1 large clove garlic, crushed

½ tsp/2.5 ml oregano

½ tsp/2.5 ml cinnamon

¼ pint/150 ml red wine

salt and pepper to taste

6 oz/175 g wholewheat macaroni

topping:

2 eggs, size 3

¾ pint/450 ml white sauce

4 oz/125 g Cheddar cheese, grated

Preheat the oven to Gas Mark 6/400F/200C.

Chop the onions, peppers and mushrooms. Heat the oil in a large saucepan and add the crushed garlic. Add the onion and fry until soft and golden. Add the peppers, stir and continue frying for about 6 minutes until soft. Add the mushrooms, stir and continue frying for a further 2–3 minutes. Add the tomatoes and all their juice, the drained lentils, the herbs, cinnamon and wine. Bring to the boil, stirring all the time, then simmer, covered, for about 15 minutes until the lentils are soft. Season to taste with salt and pepper.

While the lentil sauce is simmering, cook the macaroni in boiling salted water until tender. Prepare the white sauce and allow to cool for 2 minutes. Beat the eggs one at a time into the white sauce. Drain the macaroni and arrange in the bottom of an ovenproof dish. Pour the lentil sauce mixture over the macaroni. Pour over the white sauce. Sprinkle with the grated cheese. Bake in the oven for 40 minutes, until the topping has risen and is golden brown. Serve immediately.

Cheesy Spirals

Serves: 4
Prep: 10 mins
Cook: 15 mins

Linda Springett from Camberley, Surrey, says this is her family's favourite supper dish. It's certainly perfect for children who are reluctant meat eaters!

8 oz/225 g pasta spirals

2 medium courgettes

2 medium broccoli heads

2 oz/50 g sunflower margarine

2 oz/50 g wholewheat flour

1 pint/600 ml semi-skimmed milk

6 oz/175 g strong Cheddar cheese, grated

8 oz/226 g can kidney beans

1 tbsp/15 ml sesame seeds

Cook the pasta in boiling salted water until just tender.

Meanwhile slice the courgettes and break the broccoli into small florets. Blanch in a pan of boiling water for 5 minutes.

Melt the margarine in a saucepan, remove from the heat and slowly stir in the flour. Cook for 1 minute. Gradually add the milk and when all is added replace on the heat and bring to the boil, stirring all the time. When simmering add most of the cheese to the sauce. Drain pasta and place in a heatproof dish. Add the drained vegetables and the kidney beans. Pour the cheese sauce over the other ingredients and stir gently. Sprinkle the remaining cheese and sesame seeds over the top and brown under a hot grill. Serve immediately.

Variation: Use your favourite vegetables.

Courgette Loaf

Serves: 4–6
Prep: 10 mins
Cook: 50–60 mins

This unusual courgette loaf by Caroline Chambers of Fareham, Hampshire, looks wonderful and tastes smashing. Serve it in thin slices with crusty bread as a starter or more generous helpings with salad for a delicious lunch.

2½ lb/1.1 kg courgettes

3 medium onions

8 cloves garlic

1 tbsp/15 ml butter

6 eggs

4 fl oz/113 ml carton cream or fromage frais

2 tbsp/30 ml parsley, chopped

pinch nutmeg

salt and pepper

Preheat the oven to Gas Mark 4/350F/180C. Grease a 1 lb/450 g loaf tin.

Wash the courgettes and slice thinly. Steam them until tender for about 7–10 minutes. Drain in a large sieve and crush them with a fork to get rid of excess moisture.

Chop the onions and garlic. Heat the butter in a saucepan and fry them gently until soft. Place in a liquidiser or food processor and blend until smooth.

Beat the eggs and add the cream or fromage frais and the chopped parsley. Add the courgettes, onion and garlic mixture to the eggs and cream and mix altogether. Add the nutmeg and salt and pepper to taste. Pour the mixture into the tin and cover with foil. Place the tin in a roasting pan half filled with water. Place the pan in the oven and bake for 50–60 minutes until firm. Remove from tin while still warm and leave to cool. Serve chilled and cut into slices.

Vegetable Curry, Aduki Bean Moussaka, Courgette Loaf and Stuffed Aubergine

Aduki Bean Moussaka

Serves: 4–6
Prep: 15 mins
**Cook: 1 hour 40
mins**

cheese sauce:

1 oz/25 g butter

1 oz/25 g cornflour

¾ pint/450 ml milk

**4 oz/125 g Cheddar
cheese, grated**

moussaka filling:

2 tbsp/30 ml oil

2 potatoes, thinly sliced

2 medium onions

2 courgettes

**6 oz/175 g mushrooms,
chopped**

2 cloves garlic

4 oz/125 g aduki beans

**15 oz/425 g can
tomatoes**

**¼ pint/150 ml vegetable
stock**

**2 tbsp/30 ml tomato
purée**

2 tbsp/30 ml soy sauce

½ tsp/2.5 ml oregano

salt and pepper to taste

*This robust, hearty moussaka-style dish from
C. Downton of Melksham, Wiltshire, is a
marvellous winter warmer and one the
whole family will love.*

Soak the aduki beans in boiling water for 1 hour,
bring to the boil and simmer for 1 hour. Preheat
the oven to Gas Mark 6/400F/200C.

Make up the sauce by melting the butter in a
saucepan. Remove from the heat and stir in cornflour. Gradually add the milk, stirring continuously, then return to heat. Continue stirring until
the sauce begins to thicken. Remove from the heat
and mix in the cheese and leave to cool.

Heat half the oil in a frying pan and fry the
potatoes until lightly browned. Drain on kitchen
paper then line the sides and base of a casserole
dish with the potatoes.

To make the filling chop the vegetables, heat the
remaining oil in a large pan and fry the onions,
courgettes, mushrooms and garlic for 2 minutes.
Add the drained aduki beans and cook for a
further 3 minutes. Pour in the tomatoes, stock,
tomato purée and soy sauce. Season with oregano,
salt and pepper. Simmer for 10 minutes. Spoon
the mixture over the potatoes and then pour the
cheese sauce over the top. Cook in the oven for 20
minutes then serve with crusty bread.

Stuffed Aubergines

Serves: 4
Prep: 15 mins
Cook: 40 mins

Claire de Carle of Amersham, Buckinghamshire, suggests you serve these golden cheese-topped stuffed aubergines with salad for lunch or rice for a more substantial vegetarian dinner.

2 medium aubergines

salt

4 fl oz/100 ml olive oil

1 onion, chopped

8 oz/225 g mushrooms, chopped

3 tbsp/45 ml fresh parsley, chopped

4 oz/125 g low-fat soft cheese

2 oz/50 g breadcrumbs

2 oz/50 g vegetarian Cheddar cheese, grated

salt and pepper

Preheat the oven to Gas Mark 4/350F/180C.

Cut the aubergines in half lengthways and scoop out the flesh with a spoon, taking care to leave the skin and some flesh intact. Sprinkle each half generously with salt. Leave for 30 minutes. Rinse the aubergine skins thoroughly and dry on kitchen paper.

Heat half the oil in a large frying pan and fry the skins for approximately 2 minutes on each side. Remove and place in an ovenproof dish.

Chop the flesh from the aubergine into small pieces. Heat the other half of the oil and fry the onion with the aubergine flesh for 4 minutes. Add the mushrooms and continue cooking for a further 3 minutes. Remove from the heat and add the remaining ingredients except the grated cheese and mix together. Pile the stuffing into the aubergine skins. Sprinkle with grated cheese and bread crumbs and place in the oven for 20 minutes until cheese turns golden brown.

This is delicious served with a spicy tomato sauce and crusty rolls as a snack or as a main course with rice and sweetcorn.

Tip: If you haven't time to make your own sauce, buy one of the ready-made tomato sauces now available.

Vegetable Curry

Serves: 4–6
Prep: 15 mins
Cook: 20 mins

One of the most gorgeous vegetable curries we've ever tasted. Iris Henn from Salt in Stafford adds desiccated coconut, sultanas and peanuts to this exotic version.

1 tbsp/15 ml oil

2 large onions

1 small green pepper

2 carrots

1 celery stick

3 tomatoes

1 tbsp/15 ml lemon juice

1 large eating apple, peeled, cored and chopped

1 oz/25 g dark brown sugar

2 tbsp/30 ml mild curry powder

2 tsp/10 ml turmeric

2 tbsp/30 ml desiccated coconut

2 tbsp/30 ml sultanas

1 oz/25 g plain flour

½ pint/300 ml vegetable stock

1 oz/25 g peanuts

salt and pepper to taste

Chop the onions, green peppers, carrots and celery. Heat the oil in a large pan and add the vegetables. Cook gently for 5 minutes until softened. Skin and chop the tomatoes and peel, core and chop the apple. Add the tomatoes, lemon juice, apple, sugar, curry powder, turmeric, coconut and sultanas. Stir in the flour and vegetable stock and season to taste. Cook gently for 15–20 minutes, until the vegetables are softened but not mushy. Add the peanuts and heat through for 1 minute. Serve with rice.

Microwave Tip:
Place the oil, green pepper, carrots and celery in a large bowl. Cover and cook for 5 minutes on high. Stir in the onions, tomatoes, lemon juice, apple, sugar, curry powder, turmeric and coconut. Cover and cook on high for a further 10 minutes. Stir twice, then stir in the flour, hot stock, sultanas, peanuts, salt and pepper. Cover and cook for 4 minutes, stirring halfway through.

Main Courses

Shahi Murghi
(Royal Chicken)

Serves: 6–8
Prep: 20 mins
Cook: 50 mins

3 lb/1.4 kg chicken or chicken pieces

juice from 2 limes

2 tbsp/30 ml salt

½ tsp/2.5 ml saffron strands

1 tbsp/15 ml warm milk

yellow food colouring

2–4 tbsp/30–60 ml oil

1 onion, thinly sliced

8–10 cloves garlic

2 in/5 cm fresh ginger

2 tsp/10 ml ground coriander

2 tsp/10 ml chilli powder

4 oz/125 g flaked almonds

½ tsp/2.5 ml garam masala

2 oz/50 g raisins

Sabiha Ahmed from Taunton in Somerset has modified a very lavish Indian dish and created a recipe truly fit for a princess.

Preheat the oven to Gas Mark 5/375F/190C.

Cut the chicken into small pieces and remove the skin. Prick the meat with a fork and rub with lime juice and salt. Leave for 20 minutes.

Mix the saffron with the milk and leave to infuse, add a few drops of yellow colouring to get a good colour. Brush the chicken pieces with mixture.

Heat the oil in a frying pan and fry the onions until brown. Put the ginger, garlic, coriander, chilli and half the almonds in a food processor. Add 1 tbsp/15 ml water and mix to a paste. Add the paste to the onions and cook until the mixture looks crumbly. Add the garam masala. Stir in the chicken and mix well. Transfer to an ovenproof casserole and sprinkle with remaining almonds and raisins. Cover and cook in the oven for 50 minutes. Serve with Basmati rice or naan bread.

Herbed Chicken in Coconut Milk

Serves: 4
Prep: 10 mins
Cook: 10–15 mins

1 oz/25 g fresh ginger, peeled

7 cloves garlic, peeled

1 tbsp/15 ml ground coriander

4 peppercorns

2 lemon grass stems

3 shallots, peeled

5 chillies, deseeded

4 tbsp/60 ml oyster sauce

4 tbsp/60 ml lime juice

12 fl oz/350 ml coconut milk

1 lb/450 g chicken breast, thinly sliced

A chicken dish with a true Thai flavour. Check out your local Chinese food shops for ingredients. From Mrs Jacqueline Schou, London.

Liquidise or pound half the ginger, with the garlic, coriander, peppercorns, lemon grass, shallots, chillies, oyster sauce and lime juice until it is a thick paste.

Bring 4 fl oz/100 ml of the coconut milk to the boil in a saucepan. Add the paste and the chicken. Shred the remaining ginger and add with the remaining coconut milk. Cook until the chicken is tender, about 10–15 minutes. Serve in a bowl with Basmati rice.

Tip: To make coconut milk either buy a block of creamed coconut and melt down, or infuse 4 oz/125 g desiccated coconut in 12 fl oz/350 ml boiling water for 30 minutes. Press through a sieve, to strain coconut.

Over the page: clockwise from top left: Benedictine Chicken, Herbed Chicken in Coconut Milk, Spicy Coated Leg of Lamb, Royal Chicken, and Tandoori Chicken with Green Bananas

Tandoori Chicken with Green Bananas

Serves: 6
Prep: 15 mins
Cook: 1 hour 15 mins

If you've never made Tandoori chicken before then try this easy-to-follow recipe by Pragna Raval from London.

2 tsp/10 ml fresh ginger

2 tsp/10 ml fresh green chillis

2 tbsp/30 ml Tandoori paste

1 tsp/5 ml turmeric

2 tsp/10 ml chilli powder

2 tsp/10 ml salt

1 tbsp/15 ml fresh coriander, chopped

5 fl oz/125 ml natural yoghurt

6 chicken pieces

5 small potatoes

1 oz/25 g flour

1 tbsp/15 ml milk

oil for frying

2 green bananas

Preheat the oven to Gas Mark 6/400F/200C.

Peel and grate the ginger, deseed and chop the chillis and thickly slice the potatoes. Mix together the Tandoori paste, spices, herbs and yoghurt in a bowl. Add the chicken and potatoes, making sure they are well covered with the mixture. Cover and refrigerate overnight. Remove the chicken and potatoes from the marinade, using a slotted spoon so that not too much liquid is removed. Place in a roasting dish and cook for about 1 hour.

Peel and thickly slice the bananas. Mix together the flour and milk, dip the banana into the mixture. Heat the oil in a frying pan. Fry the battered bananas until golden brown all over. Serve the chicken surrounded by the potatoes and fried bananas.

Benedictine Curried Chicken

Serves: 4–6
Prep: 25 mins
Cook: 25 mins

This mild chicken curry makes a wonderful centre piece for a dinner party. Mr A. Anderson of Newton Stewart serves it on a bed of fragrant apricot and chestnut rice.

5 chicken breast fillets

2 oz/50 g butter

2 large onions, sliced

2 tsp/10 ml curry powder

1 pint/600 ml chicken stock

2 tbsp/30 ml plain flour

7 fl oz/200 ml double cream

2 tbsp/30 ml brandy

3 oz/75 g dried apricots

6 tbsp/90 ml white wine

¾ pint/450 ml water

1 chicken stock cube

1 tsp/5 ml turmeric

3 oz/75 g brown rice

3 oz/75 g white rice

8 oz/226 g can waterchestnuts

3 spring onions

1 tbsp/15 ml parsley

1 red pepper

Cut the chicken into thin strips. Melt half the butter in a frying pan. Add the chicken and stir-fry until slightly browned. Remove from pan. Add remaining butter and fry the onion until golden brown. Stir in curry powder and cook for 1 minute. Add chicken stock. Mix the flour with 4 tbsp/60 ml water and add to pan. Stir in the cream, bring to the boil and stir until the sauce thickens and reduces slightly. Stir in the brandy and add the chicken. Cook for 20 minutes while cooking rice.

For the rice, chop the apricots and soak in the wine for 15–20 minutes. Bring ¾ pint/450 ml water to the boil and add the stock cube, turmeric and brown rice. Boil uncovered for 20 minutes. Add the white rice, boiling until both rices are cooked (about 10 minutes). Drain rice and mix well with apricot mixture. Slice the water-chestnuts and chop the spring onions, parsley and red pepper. Add to the rice and serve with the chicken.

Spicy Coated Leg of Lamb

Serves: 6–8
Prep: 10 mins
Cook: 2 hours

You may never have thought of spicing lamb in this way but it's definitely worth trying. A smashing recipe from Mrs Ismat Parkar of Rise Park in Nottingham.

4 lb/1.8 kg leg of lamb

3 green chillies

14 oz/400 g natural yoghurt

1 tsp/5 ml turmeric

2 tbsp/30 ml ground cumin

2 tbsp/30 ml garam masala

2 tbsp/30 ml fresh coriander leaves

2 tbsp/30 ml chilli powder

2 tbsp/30 ml ground ginger

2 cloves garlic, crushed

Preheat the oven to Gas Mark 4/350F/180C.

Prick the skin of the lamb with a fork and place in a roasting pan. Deseed and finely chop the chillis and crush the garlic cloves. In a bowl combine all the ingredients and mix well. Spread the mixture thickly all over the leg of lamb, cover with foil and place in the oven. Cook for about 2 hours. Serve with rice and garnish with fresh coriander.

Tip: For a stronger flavour, cover the lamb with the yoghurt mixture and marinade over-night, then cook as above.

For a more economical version use shoulder of lamb.

Medallions of Veal and Elizabeth's Raspberry Duck

Huntsmans Loaf

Serves: 6–8
Prep: 10 mins
Cook: 1–1½ hours

Mr Philip Hunt from Wallington, Surrey, won a place in this book for his very flavoursome meat loaf recipe. It makes a delicious lunch dish.

1 small onion

2 oz/50 g mushrooms

half green pepper

1½ lb/700 g minced beef

4 tbsp/60 ml breadcrumbs

1 egg

¼ pint/150 ml milk

2 cloves garlic, crushed

8 oz/225 g can tomatoes

salt and pepper

Preheat the oven to Gas Mark 4/350F/180C.

Finely chop the onion and mushrooms and deseed and chop the pepper. Combine all the ingredients in a large bowl. Mix well. Season lightly. Spoon the mixture into a lightly greased 1 lb/450 g loaf tin. Smooth the surface with the back of a spoon. Cook for 1–1½ hours, or until firm to the touch and well browned.

When cooked remove from tin, place on serving plate and serve with Jersey new potatoes, petit pois and fresh asparagus.

Medallions of Veal

Serves: 2
Prep: 5 mins
Cook: 10 mins

A really fast to cook recipe, but one that's grand enough for those most special occasions. From Mrs G. M. Riding of Emsworth, Hampshire.

2 tbsp/30 ml olive oil

1 oz/25 g butter

2 veal fillets

1 onion, chopped

4 oz/125 g button mushrooms

¼ pint/150 ml double cream

4 tbsp/60 ml port

2 slices ham

Heat the oil and butter in frying pan, and when sizzling fry veal fillets on both sides for about 5 minutes. Remove with a slotted spoon and keep warm.

Fry the onions and mushrooms in the same oil for about 7 minutes until soft. Stir in the cream, port, seasoning and chopped ham and simmer for a few minutes to heat through. Pour the sauce over cooked veal fillet and serve with rice and vegetables.

Elizabeth's Raspberry Duck

Serves: 8
Prep: 10 mins
Cook: 25 mins

8 plump duck breasts

salt

1 lb/450 g fresh or frozen raspberries, defrosted

¼ pint/150 ml white wine vinegar

2 tbsp/30 ml brown sugar

1 pint/600 ml chicken stock

1 tbsp/15 ml butter, softened

1 tbsp/15 ml flour

Elizabeth Cope from Whetstone, London, has created this really lovely dinner party dish. It makes duck deliciously different.

Preheat the oven to Gas Mark 6/400F/200C.

Rub the skin on each breast with a thick layer of salt to absorb the fat and leave the skin crispy. Place on a rack in a roasting tin and cook for 25 minutes in the oven.

Push half the raspberries through a fine sieve. Discard the pips. Mix the sieved fruit with the vinegar and brown sugar. Heat gently in a saucepan until the sugar dissolves. Bring to the boil and reduce until you have a thick syrup. Carefully add the stock, being careful not to scald your fingers on any steam and simmer for a few minutes. Mix together the butter and flour and stir into the sauce to thicken it. Season and add raspberries.

Remove the duck from the oven and brush off the salt. Slice the breasts and arrange on a serving plate. Pour over the sauce and serve with vegetables.

Venison Carbonade

Serves: 6
Prep: 10 mins
Cook: 3 hours

2 lb/900 g venison shoulder, boned

4 tbsp/60 ml oil

1 large onion, chopped

1 clove garlic, crushed

4 oz/125 g mushrooms

2 oz/50 g streaky bacon, diced

1 bouquet garni

3 tbsp/45 ml flour

½ pint/300 ml beef stock

½ pint/300 ml brown ale

2 tbsp/30 ml wine vinegar

1 tbsp/15 ml brown sugar

salt and pepper

This recipe is a family special from Mrs Veronica Heath of Morpeth, Northumberland. Her father, husband and two sons are deer-stalkers and she uses venison regularly.

Preheat the oven to Gas Mark 4/350F/180C.

Trim and cut the meat into cubes. Heat the oil in a frying pan and brown the meat. Transfer to a casserole dish.

In the same frying pan lightly brown the onion, garlic and mushrooms. Set aside for later. Brown the bacon and add to the meat in the casserole dish.

Add the bouquet garni to the juices in the frying pan and stir in the flour. Gradually add the stock, ale and vinegar and bring the sauce to the boil. Season with sugar, salt and pepper. Pour the sauce over the meat, cover and cook for 1 hour.

Reduce heat to Gas Mark 3/325F/160C. Add the cooked onions, garlic and mushrooms and cook for a further 2 hours. Serve with baked potatoes.

Tip: This stew is also lovely made with beef.

From top, clockwise: Venison Carbonade, Huntsmans Loaf and Rabbit Casserole

Rabbit Casserole

Serves: 4–6
Prep: 10 mins
Cook: 1½ hours

This delicious meat is available in supermarkets everywhere and makes a tempting and delicious casserole. Margaret Lipke-Coates from Appledore, Devon, cooks rabbit in white wine for extra flavour.

1 savoy cabbage, shredded

2 tbsp/30 ml oil

1 oz/25 g butter

1 lb/450 g rabbit pieces or 1 rabbit, jointed

1 tbsp/15 ml parsley, chopped

2 cloves garlic, thinly sliced

¼ pint/150 ml dry white wine (Muscadet)

4–6 rashers bacon

Preheat the oven to Gas Mark 4/350F/180C.

Place the cabbage in the base of a greased casserole dish.

Heat the oil and butter in a large frying pan and fry the rabbit pieces until golden. Arrange rabbit on top of cabbage and sprinkle over parsley and garlic.

Add 4 tbsp/60 ml water to the frying pan with the wine, bring to the boil, then pour over rabbit. The liquid should just cover the cabbage, add more wine if necessary. Cover with bacon rashers. Replace lid and bake for 1 hour.

Remove lid and cook for another ½ hour to crisp bacon. Serve with baked potatoes, glazed carrots and seasonal salad.

Tip: To make easy glazed carrots, place 1 lb/450 g sliced carrots in a large saucepan and just cover with water. Add a pinch of salt, 1 tsp/5 ml brown sugar and 1 tsp/5 ml butter. Bring to the boil, uncovered, and simmer until the liquid has reduced. The remaining sugar and butter mixture will start to brown the carrots. Toss the carrots in this mixture until evenly coated, just browned but not burnt.

Salmon Surprise

Serves: 4–6
Prep: 30 mins
Cook: 40 mins

This recipe looks very classy and tastes it too. Mrs Hester Wood from Nercwys, Clwyd, makes it economical by using a salmon tail piece.

2 oz/50 g butter

2 oz/50 g raisins

2 oz/50 g blanched almonds

4 pieces stem ginger

10 asparagus spears

2½ lb/1.1 kg salmon

salt and black pepper

1 lb/450 g shortcrust pastry

beaten egg, to glaze

herb & lemon sauce:

2 oz/50 g butter

2 shallots

1 tsp/5 ml chervil

1 tsp/5 ml tarragon

1 tsp/5 ml parsley

1 tsp/5 ml plain flour

½ pint/300 ml single cream

1 tsp/5 ml Dijon mustard

2 egg yolks

juice of one lemon

salt and pepper

Preheat the oven to Gas Mark 4/350F/180C.

Chop the almonds and ginger and blanch the asparagus.

Mix together the butter, raisins, almonds and ginger, and spread half the mixture on to a skinned and boned salmon fillet. Sandwich together with the other fillet. Spread the remaining mixture on top. Top with asparagus spears and season well.

Divide the pastry in two and roll out on a floured surface, to make two 8 × 6 in/20 × 15 cm rectangles, large enough to enclose the salmon. Place the salmon on the centre of pastry and brush pastry edge with glaze. Top with the remaining pastry. Press edges together to seal firmly. Trim parcel into oval shape and crimp the edges. Re-roll trimmings and cut out fish shapes to decorate pastry. Make a few slashes in the pastry, brush with remaining egg glaze and bake for 30–35 minutes until well risen and brown.

Meanwhile make the sauce. Melt the butter in a pan, add the finely chopped shallots and herbs and lightly fry until soft. Stir in the flour, cream and seasoning. Simmer for 10 minutes and then cool. Add the egg yolk to the cream mixture. Simmer over a low heat until ready to serve. Do not boil. Add lemon juice to taste.

Serve the salmon with the sauce and garnish with fennel leaves and lemon twists.

Fillet of Pork Parcels with Apple Rings

Serves: 4–6
Prep: 40 mins
Cook: 1–1½ hours

2 lb/900 g pork fillet

2 oz/50 g butter for roasting

¼ pint/150 ml stock

¼ pint/150 ml beer

2 Cox's apples

8 tbsp/120 ml redcurrant jelly to glaze

watercress for garnish

stuffing:

6 oz/175 g minced pork

8 oz/225 g sausagemeat

4 oz/125 g liver, minced

4 oz/125 g cooked ham, minced

seasoning:

1 tbsp/15 ml parsley and sage, chopped

grated rind and juice half lemon

3 tbsp/45 ml breadcrumbs

1 egg, beaten

This earned Judith Archer of Kings Bromley, Burton-on-Trent, the title 'Cook of the County'. It's a marvellous dinner party recipe.

Preheat the oven to Gas Mark 6/400F/200C.

Divide the pork fillet into four. Slice the fillets in half lengthways, turn cut side down and beat out flat between oiled paper using a steak hammer (or rolling pin).

Prepare the stuffing by mixing all those ingredients together. Season.

Put a quarter of the stuffing in the centre of each fillet and form a parcel. Tuck the edges underneath and secure with string. Place in a roasting tin and spread over 2 oz/50 g butter and half the stock and beer. Roast, uncovered, for 1–1½ hours, basting frequently.

Make gravy from the juices in the pan and the extra stock, thickened if wished. Add a little extra beer to flavour.

Peel, core and slice the apples in 4 and fry in butter turning once until cooked.

When the meat is cooked and well browned take up, remove string, glaze with the jelly and arrange on a serving platter with the fried apple rings and garnish with sage.

Salmon Surprise and Fillet of Pork Parcels with Apple Rings

Taylor Toad Supreme

Serves: 4
Prep: 10 mins
Cook: 30–40 mins

Eleven-year-old Mark Taylor from Daventry William Parker School, Northants, has sent in a really original recipe for Toad in the Hole – all the judges loved it!

¼ tsp/1.25 ml salt

freshly ground black pepper

4 oz/125 g flour

1 egg

4 fl oz/100 ml milk

3 drops tabasco

1 tbsp/15 ml vegetable fat

filling:

1 lb/450 g pork sausages

8 oz/225 g button mushrooms, quartered

1 onion, chopped

paprika

½ tsp/2.5 ml fresh or dried mixed herbs, chopped

1 green pepper

Preheat the oven to Gas Mark 6/400F/200C.

First make the batter. Put the salt and black pepper in a mixing bowl with the flour. With a wooden spoon beat in the egg and gradually beat in enough milk to form a smooth batter. Put the batter aside for 5 minutes. Add the tabasco to the milk that's left over, and gradually add the remaining milk, beating constantly. Cover and put to one side.

Place the fat in a medium sized baking dish and place the dish in the oven for 5 minutes.

Remove and place the sausages, mushrooms, green pepper and onion in the dish, and sprinkle paprika and mixed herbs over sausages. Put the dish back in the oven for 10–15 minutes, turning the sausages occasionally or until they are cooked and crisp.

Take dish from oven and add the batter. Turn down the oven to a moderate heat Gas Mark 4/350F/180C. Cook for about 30–40 minutes, or until the batter is risen and golden brown. Take dish from oven and serve immediately.

Pork with Beer Sauce

Serves: 4
Prep: 10 mins
Cook: 1½ hours

Beer makes the most wonderful sauce to accompany meat of all kinds. Mavis Wheeler of Northampton serves her beer sauce with loin of pork.

1¾ lb/800 g loin of pork in one piece

salt and pepper to taste

1 garlic clove, crushed

2 tbsp/30 ml vegetable oil

2 small onions, quartered

¾ pint/450 ml Newcastle Brown or Guinness

¼ pint/5 fl oz/142 ml carton single cream

1 tbsp/15 ml cornflour

Trim the meat of all fat. Rub the meat with seasoning and garlic. Heat the oil in a large heat-proof casserole and add the meat. Fry until browned on all sides, then add the onions and brown lightly. Pour in the beer and stir well. Cover and simmer gently for 1½ hours, basting meat with beer every 20–30 minutes. To test if meat is cooked, pierce deeply with a metal skewer, if the juices run clear, remove from the casserole and place on a warmed serving dish. Slice thickly.

Blend the cream and cornflour together and stir into the beer liquid. Bring to the boil and stir until thick and smooth. Season to taste with salt and pepper and strain. Serve the meat with red or green cabbage, boiled with apple and caraway seeds.

Mustard and Apple Lamb Chops

Serves: 4
Prep: 10 mins
Cook: 30–35 mins

1 tbsp/15 ml vegetable oil

1 onion, chopped

1 tomato, sliced

2 cloves garlic, crushed

8 lamb chops

3 tbsp/45 ml dijon mustard

8 fl oz/250 ml apple juice

¼ pint/150 ml chicken stock

freshly ground black pepper

Here's a really different way to serve lamb chops from Mrs J. Snow, Stowmarket, Suffolk.

Heat the oil in a large frying pan. Add the onion, tomato and garlic and fry for about 7 minutes until soft. Add the chops and brown on both sides.

In a bowl mix together the mustard, apple juice and stock. Season with the pepper. Add to pan and stir well. Cover and cook for 15 minutes. Remove lid and cook on high heat for 10 minutes to reduce the sauce. Serve with potatoes and vegetables of your choice.

Tip: Apple juice makes a good substitute for wine.

Tarragon Lamb Bake, Pork 'n' Cider, Mustard and Apple Lamb Chops, Pork with Beer Sauce and Taylor Toad Supreme

Tarragon Lamb Bake

Serves: 4
Prep: 10 mins
Cook: 20–25 mins

Jon de Vries from Chelmsford, Essex, makes clever use of the minced lamb you find in so many supermarkets now.

2 tbsp/30 ml oil

1 onion, finely chopped

1 lb/450 g minced lamb

1 lamb stock cube

1 tbsp/15 ml dried tarragon

salt and black pepper

1 tsp/5 ml cornflour (optional)

topping:

3 oz/75 g butter

6 oz/175 g flour

2 oz/50 g mature Cheddar, grated

2 tsp/10 ml tarragon

3 oz/75 g breadcrumbs

Preheat the oven to Gas Mark 6/400F/200C.

Heat oil in a large frying pan and add the onion. Cook until brown and soft. Stir in mince and brown. Crumble in stock cube with ½ pint/300 ml boiling water, tarragon and seasoning. Stir in the cornflour to thicken if necessary.

To make the topping, rub the butter into the flour until it resembles breadcrumbs. Stir in the cheese, tarragon and breadcrumbs. Spoon mince into 1 pint/600 ml ovenproof dish. Sprinkle over topping and bake for 20–25 minutes until golden brown. Serve immediately.

Microwave Tip:
Place the onion and oil in dish, cover and microwave high for 4 minutes. Stir in the mince and cook on high for 4 minutes. Add stock, cool for remaining 1 minute.

Pork 'n' Cider

Serves: 4
Prep: 10 mins
Cook: 45 mins

Lillian Ross-MacKenzie from Stirchley, Birmingham, says her guests just can't wait to eat this delicious casserole – 'The aroma of apples and onions sizzling in hot cider is just too much to resist.'

2 oz/50 g butter

4 lean pork chops

1 onion, sliced

1 lb/450 g cooking apples, peeled and sliced

¾ pint/450 ml dry cider

salt and pepper

sage leaves to garnish

Basmati rice, to serve

Preheat the oven to Gas Mark 4/350F/180C.

Melt the butter in a frying pan and brown the chops. Place in an ovenproof casserole dish.

Fry the onions and sliced apples until golden and spoon over chops. Pour in cider and season with salt and pepper. Replace lid and bake in oven for 35–45 minutes until the meat is cooked. Garnish with sage leaves and serve with cooked Basmati rice.

Salmon Fish Cakes

Serves: 4–6
Prep: 10 mins
Cook: 15 mins

15 oz/425 g can pink
salmon, drained

1 tbsp/15 ml lemon juice

14 oz/400 g packet
mashed potato or frozen
mashed potato

6 spring onions, trimmed
and chopped

3 oz/75 g Cheddar
cheese, grated

1 tsp/5 ml dried parsley

1 egg, beaten

2 oz/50 g wholemeal
flour

salt and pepper

coating:

2 oz/50 g plain flour

2 eggs, beaten

4 oz/100 g breadcrumbs

½ pint/300 ml oil for
frying

It's definitely worth making your own fish cakes – they taste so much nicer than the frozen kind! Here's a great recipe from Mrs B. R. Whitehead of Greenhithe in Kent.

Combine the salmon, lemon juice, potato, spring onions, cheese, parsley, egg and flour in a bowl and season lightly.

Divide the mixture into 6 equal parts. Shape into thick patties.

For the coating, dip each patty into the flour then the egg and finally completely cover with breadcrumbs. Heat the oil in a deep frying pan. When hot deep fry each patty for about 3 minutes. Serve immediately.

Tip: These cakes freeze very well and can be cooked straight from frozen, but allow longer to cook.

Seafood Lasagne, Stewkey Seafood Cobbler, Flaky Fish Surprise and Salmon Fish Cakes

Seafood Lasagne

Serves: 4–6
Prep: 45 mins
Cook: 40 mins

4 oz/125 g butter

1 onion, finely chopped

12 oz/350 g haddock fillets, skinned and chopped

8 oz/225 g cod fillets, skinned and chopped

4 oz/125 g frozen prawns, defrosted

4 oz/125 g button mushrooms, sliced

14 oz/396 g can tomatoes

4 tsp/20 ml tomato purée

½ tsp/2.5 ml dried marjoram

4 tbsp/60 ml flour

1¾ pint/1 litre semi-skimmed milk

3 bay leaves

6–8 sheets ready cooked lasagne

pinch mace

1 tbsp/15 ml fresh dill, chopped

Mrs M. Law from Bideford, Devon, sent us this brilliantly simple seafood lasagne recipe. Layers of pasta simply bursting with fish, prawns and herb flavoured vegetables – delicious!

Preheat the oven to Gas Mark 5/375F/190C.

Melt 1 oz/25 g butter and fry the onion for about 7 minutes until soft. Add the fish. Stir in the prawns and cook for about 5 minutes until the fish is soft but not browned. Add the mushrooms, tomatoes, purée and herbs. Simmer on a low heat for 5 minutes.

Bring the milk and the bay leaves to the boil and remove from the heat.

Heat the remaining butter in a saucepan. Add the flour and mace and mix well. Gradually add the milk, bring to the boil and stir until thick. Layer an ovenproof dish first with lasagne then fish mixture and white sauce. Sprinkle the top with fresh dill. Cook for 20–25 minutes until bubbly. Serve immediately.

Tip: If you like, add 4 oz/125 g cheese for an extra-tasty sauce.

Flaky Fish Surprise

Serves: 4
Prep: 20 mins
Cook: 15–20 mins

Fifteen-year-old Paul Woodward of Redworth, County Durham, described his recipe perfectly. 'An elegantly light parcel of filo pastry filled with white fish, prawns and a delicate herb sauce.' Need we say more!

¼ oz/15 g butter

¼ oz/15 g flour

¼ pint/150 ml milk

salt and pepper

1 tbsp/15 ml parsley, chopped

1 tbsp/15 ml dill, chopped

12 sheets filo pastry

4 oz/125 g butter

4 oz/125 g prawns

4 plaice fillets

Preheat the oven to Gas Mark 4/350F/180C.

First make a white sauce. Place the butter, flour, milk and seasoning in a pan and bring to the boil, whisking all the time. Simmer for 2 minutes until thick. Stir in the parsley. Allow to cool.

Melt the remaining butter. Brush 3 sheets of filo pastry with the butter and layer on top of each other. Repeat with remaining pastry so you have 4 pastry squares.

Divide the prawns between the 4 fillets and roll each fillet to enclose prawns. Place one fillet on each pastry square and spoon the thickened sauce over each fillet. Top with dill. Gather the four corners of the pastry to the centre and seal together to form a purse with a frilly top. Repeat with 3 other pieces. Place on a greased baking sheet, bake for 15–20 minutes until golden brown. Serve immediately with julienne of carrot and courgette or mange-tout.

Variations:
Replace plaice for sole, haddock or other white fish. Vary herbs and use a light lemon sauce. Tie a piece of chive round each parcel before serving.

Stewkey Sea Food Cobbler

Serves: 4
Prep: 30 mins
Cook: 20 mins

It's extra special when recipes feature regional specialities. T. J. Davy of Dereham, Norfolk, includes stewkey blues, large cockles from Stiffkey on the Norfolk coast.

1 lb/450 g smoked haddock or cod

½ pint/300 ml milk

¼ pint/150 ml dry white wine

1 oz/25 g butter

1 oz/25 g plain flour

1 tsp/5 ml mustard

2 oz/50 g cheese, grated

4 oz/125 g peeled prawns

4 oz/125 g stewkey blues, boiled and shelled or cockles

salt and pepper

topping:

6 oz/175 g plain flour

1 tbsp/15 ml baking powder

2 tbsp/30 ml parsley

pinch salt

1½ oz/40 g butter

1 egg

2 tbsp/30 ml milk

Preheat the oven to Gas Mark 7/425F/220C.

Skin the fish and cut into 1 in/2.5 cm × 2 in/5 cm chunks. Poach gently in ¼ pint/150 ml milk and white wine for about 5 minutes. Strain and reserve liquid. Place fish pieces in a 2 pint/1.2 litre ovenproof serving dish.

Melt the butter in pan, stir in flour and cook for 1 minute. Gradually stir in the cooking liquid and remaining milk. Mix in the mustard, salt and pepper. Bring to the boil and simmer for 3 minutes, whisking all the time, until it thickens. Stir in the cheese, prawns and cockles. Spoon over the cooked fish.

To make the scone topping, mix the flour, baking powder, chopped parsley and salt together. Rub in the butter, until the mixture resembles breadcrumbs, then stir in beaten egg and milk and mix to form a soft dough. Turn the dough on to a floured surface. Roll out until ½ in/1.5 cm thick. Cut into 1½ in/3.5 cm circles with a pastry cutter. Arrange circles of dough around top of fish mixture. Brush tops with milk or a little beaten egg. Bake for 20–25 minutes until well risen and golden brown. Serve hot.

Chicken and Pork in Black Bean Sauce

Serves: 4
Prep: 8–10 mins
Cook: 10 mins

The unusual mix of pork, chicken and spicy black bean sauce makes Mrs S. Mathieson from Tamworth's fast and easy supper dish truly delicious.

2 chicken breast fillets

6 oz/175 g pork fillet

2 onions

1 red pepper

1 green pepper

1 tbsp/15 ml vegetable oil

1 tbsp/15 ml light soy sauce

5 oz/150 g jar blackbean sauce

1 tsp/5 ml five spices powder

4 tbsp/60 ml water

Skin and cube the chicken breasts and cube the pork. Finely chop the onions and deseed and chop the peppers. Heat the oil in a wok and when hot add the chicken and pork. Stir-fry for about 4 minutes and remove from wok.

Stir-fry the onions and pepper for 2 minutes, adding more oil if necessary. Return the meat to the wok. Stir in the soy sauce, black bean sauce, five spices and 4 tbsp/60 ml water. Mix well and leave to simmer for 3 minutes. Serve on a bed of noodles, rice or bean sprouts.

Oriental Chicken

Serves: 4
Prep: 5 mins
Cook: 10 mins

Diced chicken plus some handy store-cupboard ingredients make this speedy meal devised by Janet Hardcastle of Mitcham, Surrey.

1 tbsp/15 ml cornflour

½ tsp/2.5 ml salt

1 lb/450 g chicken breasts, diced

2 tbsp/30 ml oil

1 onion, finely chopped

1 garlic clove, crushed

½ tsp/2.5 ml ground ginger

2 tbsp/30 ml soy sauce

1 tsp/5 ml sugar

1 tbsp/15 ml tomato purée

8 oz/225 g button mushrooms, chopped

Mix the cornflour and salt together and coat the chicken. Set aside.

Heat the oil in a large frying pan and fry the onion, garlic and ginger for about 5 minutes until soft. Add the diced chicken and fry for 2–3 minutes until cooked. Stir in the mushrooms and cook for a further two minutes. Stir in soy sauce, sugar and tomato purée with a little water and bring to boil. Serve immediately with stir-fried Chinese leaves, pineapple cubes and beansprouts.

Chicken Tropical

Serves: 4–6
Prep: 10 mins
Cook: 1¼ hours

1 tbsp/15 ml vegetable oil

8 small or 4 large chicken portions

4 sticks celery

2 large onions

1 carrot

7 oz/198 g can pineapple chunks, drained

1 tbsp/15 ml sultanas

1 tsp/5 ml ground ginger

1 tbsp/15 ml brown sauce

1 tbsp/15 ml sherry

½ pint/300 ml chicken stock

1 tsp/5 ml cornflour

salt and pepper

A rich and exotic chicken casserole that's quick and easy to make for a midweek family supper. Created by Mrs Brookfield of Sheffield.

Preheat the oven to Gas Mark 5/375F/190C.

Chop the celery and onions and slice the carrots. Heat the oil in a frying pan. Fry the chicken pieces until brown. Transfer to an ovenproof casserole. Add all the remaining ingredients. Mix the cornflour with a little cold water. Add to the casserole and stir well. Cover and cook for 1 hour. Serve on a bed of rice or pasta with a green salad.

Tip: Make double the quantity and freeze in individual portions. Defrost at room temperature for 6 hours and reheat for 30–40 minutes until hot.

Over the page, clockwise from top left: Chicken and Pork in Black Bean Sauce, Spare Ribs, Paradise Pork, Oriental Chicken and Chicken Tropical

Spicy Spare Ribs

Serves: 4–6
Prep: 20 mins
Cook: 1 hour 30 mins

Finger-licking delicious! The most more-ish spare rib recipe yet. From Julie Vicary, New Romney, Kent.

marinade:

2 cloves garlic, crushed

6 tbsp/90 ml dark soy sauce

2 tsp/10 ml ground ginger

4 tbsp/60 ml golden syrup

4 lb/1.8 kg pork spare ribs

sauce:

1 tbsp/15 ml vegetable oil

1 clove garlic, crushed

2 onions, finely chopped

6 tbsp/90 ml lemon juice

4 tbsp/60 ml golden syrup

6 tbsp/90 ml Worcester sauce

6 tbsp/90 ml tomato purée

2 tsp/10 ml dried sage

In a large bowl combine the garlic, soy sauce, ginger and golden syrup. Mix well. Add the spare ribs, cover and marinade in the fridge for up to 24 hours.

Preheat the oven to Gas Mark 5/375F/190C.

Transfer the spare ribs and marinade to a roasting tin. Cook for at least 1 hour, until the meat looks really dark but not burnt.

Meanwhile heat the oil in a saucepan and fry the garlic and onion for 7 minutes until soft. Add the remaining ingredients with ¾ pint/450 ml water, cover the pan and simmer over a gentle heat for 20 minutes. Serve the spare ribs with the sauce poured over them.

Paradise Pork

Serves: 4–6
Prep: 20 mins
Cook: 1 hour

Trina Beckett from Hindon, Wiltshire, has passed this recipe on to every guest that's ever eaten it! A marvellous track record for a marvellous meal.

1 bunch spring onions

4 oz/125 g baby sweet corns, sliced thickly

half red pepper

half green pepper

1 tbsp/15 ml vegetable oil

1 lb/450 g boneless pork, cubed

1 clove garlic, crushed

1 tsp/5 ml root ginger, grated

½ pint/300 ml pineapple juice

4 tbsp/60 ml cider vinegar

3 tbsp/45 ml soy sauce

2 tbsp/30 ml tomato ketchup

1 tbsp/15 ml soft brown sugar

1 tbsp/15 ml cornflour

Preheat the oven to Gas Mark 3/325F/160C.

Trim and cut the spring onions into ½ inch lengths, thickly slice the baby sweetcorn and de-seed and dice the pepper. Heat the oil in pan and brown the pork. Remove from pan. Add the vegetables, garlic and ginger and fry for 2 minutes. Stir in the pineapple juice, vinegar, soy sauce, ketchup and sugar and add the pork. Cover and simmer for 5 minutes. Transfer the pork mixture into a casserole dish, cover and cook for 1 hour.

Mix the cornflour with 1 tbsp/15 ml cold water and stir into pork. Cook for a further 30 minutes. Serve with rice, pasta and fresh vegetables.

Tip: This recipe is just as good if you use chicken or white fish.

Spicy Beef and Pepper Hot Pot

Serves: 4
Prep: 10 mins
Cook: 1 hour 20 mins

There's nothing quite like a rich, tasty hot pot on a freezing winter day. Mr Lee Darwood from Swindon sent us this particularly spicy version. If you don't like very hot food, reduce the amount of the green chilli.

1 large onion

1 green pepper

2 green chilli peppers

1 tbsp/15 ml oil

12 oz/350 g stewing steak and kidney, cubed

1 tbsp/15 ml cornflour

1 tbsp/15 ml brown sugar

2 tbsp/30 ml tomato purée

½ tsp/2.5 ml paprika

14 oz/396 g can tomatoes

2 tsp/10 ml Worcestershire sauce

½ tsp/2.5 ml mixed herbs

½ pint/300 ml beef stock

salt and pepper

Preheat the oven to Gas Mark 4/350F/180C.

Chop the onion and deseed and chop the pepper. Heat the oil in a large frying pan. Add the onion, pepper and chillies and fry until soft. Add the meat to the onions and fry until evenly browned all over. Stir the cornflour into the meat and mix well. Add the remaining ingredients and season to taste. Cook and stir until the sauce thickens. Transfer to an ovenproof casserole and cook for 1–1½ hours in the oven. Serve with rice.

Tip: For vegetarians replace beef stock with vegetable stock and beef with mushrooms.

Spicy Beef and Pepper Hot Pot, Chilli con Carne, Stilton Stuffed Pork in Pastry and Cheesy Chicken and Leek

Chilli con Carne

Serves: 4–6
Prep: 10 mins
Cook: 1 hour

1 lb/450 g lean minced beef

1 onion, sliced

2 cloves garlic, crushed

14 oz/396 g can tomatoes

1 tbsp/15 ml tomato purée

8 oz/225 g mushrooms, sliced

14 oz/396 g can kidney beans, drained

1 tsp/5 ml garam masala

1 tsp/5 ml cumin

1 tsp/5 ml ground coriander

2 tsp/10 ml chilli powder

2 bay leaves

1 tsp/5 ml dried mixed herbs

salt and pepper

A really healthy, low fat version of a classic Chilli Con Carne recipe. Created by Angela Gilligan, Glasshoughton, West Yorkshire.

Brown the mince in its own fat. Add the onions, garlic, tomatoes, purée, mushrooms and kidney beans and mix well. Stir in all the spices and herbs. Simmer for one hour in the oven (Gas Mark 4/350F/180C) or gently on the hob. Serve with Basmati rice or pitta bread.

Tip: This recipe freezes well for up to 6 months. Defrost at room temperature for 6 hours and reheat for 30–40 minutes until hot.

Cheesy Chicken and Leek

Serves: 4
Prep: 15 mins
Cook: 20 mins

2 tbsp/30 ml vegetable oil

1 clove garlic, crushed

8 oz/225 g chicken breast, cut into strips

2 oz/50 g butter

1 lb/450 g leeks, cleaned and sliced

2 tbsp/30 ml cornflour

¾ pint/350 ml milk

salt and pepper

6 oz/175 g tagliatelle, cooked

4 oz/125 g cheddar cheese, grated

3 tbsp/45 ml wholemeal breadcrumbs

Mrs Kate Calver of Bradley Stoke South, Bristol, created this delicious recipe one evening while experimenting in the kitchen.

Preheat the oven to Gas Mark 5/375F/190C.

Heat the oil in a wok or large saucepan, add the garlic and fry for 2–3 minutes. Add the chicken pieces and cook, turning occasionally until white in colour on all sides. Remove from the wok and put aside.

Melt butter in the wok or pan and cook leeks until tender. Blend the cornflour with milk and add to the leeks, stirring continuously until thick, season and place in a shallow oval dish.

Place the chicken on top of the leeks and the tagliatelle on top of the chicken. Top with cheese and finally the breadcrumbs. Place in the oven for 20 minutes until golden brown.

Tip: For a crunchier topping add a packet of crushed potato crisps with the breadcrumbs.

Steak with Fetta Salad

Serves: 6
Prep: 10 mins
Cook: 25 mins

Mohammed Allam's recipe for melt-in-the-mouth steak with a delicious Greek-style salad was sent in by his wife Carol.

1 oz/25 g butter

6 slices lean frying steak

2 onions, chopped

4 cloves garlic, crushed

4 tomatoes, sliced

salt and pepper

salad:

1 small lettuce

6 tomatoes

2 oz/50 g fresh parsley

½ cucumber

4 oz/125 g fetta cheese

4 oz/125 g black olives

1 tbsp/15 ml olive oil

1 tsp/5 ml white wine vinegar

Heat the butter in a frying pan and when hot fry the meat for a couple of minutes on each side. Remove from heat. Add the onions, garlic and tomatoes and season to taste. Return to heat, cover and simmer gently for 25 minutes.

Meanwhile prepare the salad. Clean and chop the lettuce, slice the tomatoes and cucumber and finely chop the parsley. In a large salad bowl mix together with cubed fetta cheese and stoned black olives. Sprinkle with oil and vinegar. Mix well. Serve the steak with the salad.

Pork Thingies, Speedy Pasta, Steak with Fetta Salad and Fakenham Fricassée

Pork Thingies

Serves: 4
Prep: 5 mins
Cook: 15 mins

The title may be a bit of a joke in the Hastings household but this recipe has lots of style. A truly delicious idea from K. M. Hastings of Melksham in Wiltshire.

1 oz/25 g butter

2 cloves garlic, crushed

1 lb/450 g pork fillet

½ pint/300 ml double cream

2 tbsp/30 ml brandy

Melt the butter in a frying pan and fry the garlic until golden. Cut the pork into ½ in/1.5 cm medallions and tenderise with a cooking mallet or wooden rolling pin. Add to the garlic and fry gently, turning occasionally, for 15 minutes. Add the cream and season to taste. Stir in the brandy. Heat the sauce, but do not boil. Serve with rice.

Speedy Pasta

Serves: 4–6
Prep: 10 mins
Cook: 10 mins

Just as its name implies, one of the fastest recipes in the book and one of the tastiest too. Sent in by Sara Swift from High Bickington, Devon.

6 oz/175 g pasta twists

1 tsp/5 ml sesame oil

8 oz/225 g Dolcelatte

4 cloves garlic, crushed

5 fl oz/42 ml natural yoghurt

1 tbsp/15 ml parsley

4 slices ham, chopped

10 mushrooms, sliced

Cook the pasta in boiling salted water with the sesame oil for 10 minutes.

Gently melt the Dolcelatte cheese in a saucepan. Add the yoghurt, parsley, ham and mushrooms and heat gently. Drain the pasta and mix with the sauce. Serve with green salad.

Tip: To jazz this up for special occasions replace yoghurt with double cream and add Parmesan cheese.

Stilton Stuffed Pork in Pastry

Serves: 4
Prep: 30 mins
Cook: 50 mins

2 lb/900 g pork fillet, trimmed

1 large Bramley apple, peeled, cored and chopped

8 oz/225 g Stilton cheese, crumbled

1 medium onion, finely chopped

olive oil

1 lb/450 g packet puff pastry

1 egg, beaten

sauce:

½ pint/300 ml gravy

1 small glass port

salt and pepper

These wonderful Stilton and pork pastries can be made in advance and save you lots of time when you are preparing a dinner party. From Philip Loader, Aylesford, Kent.

Preheat the oven to Gas Mark 4/350F/180C.

Cut the pork into four pieces. With a meat tenderiser, flatten each piece to approximately 6 in/15 cm × 4 in/10 cm. Mix together the apple, Stilton and onion and divide equally between the pork fillets, spreading over one half only. Fold the fillet over and press gently. Brush with olive oil and place on a baking tray. Cover with foil and cook for 20 minutes. Remove from oven and allow to cool.

Roll out the pastry and cut in four 7 in/18 cm × 5 in/13 cm pieces. Increase the temperature of the oven to Gas Mark 6/400F/200C. Wrap each pork parcel in a piece of pastry. Seal with egg and decorate the top with pastry trimmings. Brush the top with egg. Place on a baking sheet and cook for 20–30 minutes until the pastry is golden brown. To make sauce, make up ½ pint/300 ml gravy using gravy granules. Add one small glass of port and mix well. Serve with the pork and with crisp green French beans.

Turkey Loaf

Serves: 4–6
Prep: 10 mins
Cook: 1 hour

10 oz/275 g minced turkey

5 oz/150 g smoked streaky bacon, finely chopped

1 onion, finely chopped

3 oz/75 g porridge oats

1 tbsp/15 ml tomato purée

1 tsp/5 ml dried mixed herbs

1 egg, beaten

1 chicken stock cube

Sheila Fletcher from Evanton, Ross-shire, adapted a meat loaf recipe and came up with this exciting version. Her kids simply love it!

Preheat the oven to Gas Mark 5/375F/190C.

Combine the turkey, bacon, porridge oats, onion, tomato purée, herbs and egg in a bowl. Dissolve the stock cube with 1 tbsp/15 ml boiling water and stir into the mixture. Spoon the mixture into a 1 lb/450 g loaf tin. Cook for 1 hour, remove from tin and serve hot or cold with a crisp green salad.

Garlic Chicken with Green Salad, Turkey Loaf and Cheesy Chicken

Fakenham Fricassée

Serves: 4
Prep: 10 mins
Cook: 40 mins

It's worth trying Phyllis Gant from Norfolk's recipe any time but definitely have it to hand at Christmas – it's a great way to use turkey leftovers!

½ **red pepper**

½ **green pepper**

2 oz/50 g **mushrooms**

2 oz/50 g **dried apricots**

1 **onion, sliced**

2 tbsp/30 ml **vegetable oil**

1 tsp/5 ml **garam masala**

1 oz/25 g **plain flour**

¾ pint/450 ml **chicken or turkey stock**

10 oz/275 g **cooked turkey breast, cubed**

Preheat the oven to Gas Mark 4/350F/180C.

Deseed and chop the pepper, slice the mushrooms and chop the onions and apricots. Heat the oil in a frying pan and fry the onion until soft. Add the garam masala and flour, cook for 2 minutes. Add the stock, bring to the boil and stir until thickened. Add the remaining ingredients. Transfer to an ovenproof dish, cover and cook for about 40 minutes. Serve with sauté potatoes and Brussels tips.

Tip: Any turkey meat or chicken can be used in this recipe.

Garlic Chicken

Serves: 4
Prep: 15 mins
Cook: 25 mins

8 oz/225 g carrots, cut into strips

8 oz/225 g cabbage, finely cut into strips

4 boneless chicken breasts, skinned

1 egg, beaten

2 oz/50 g plain flour

2 oz/50 g cornflour

2 tbsp/30 ml oil

4 cloves garlic, crushed

2 tbsp/30 ml fresh ginger, crushed

8 oz/225 g mushrooms, sliced

1 bunch spring onions, cut into strips

¼ pint/150 ml chicken stock

3 tbsp/45 ml white wine

1 tbsp/15 ml soy sauce

A totally scrumptious way with chicken. An easy Saturday night supper from Mrs Lin Lee of Consett, County Durham.

Cook the carrots and cabbage in boiling salted water for 5 minutes. Drain.

Dip the chicken in the beaten egg. Combine the 2 flours, and coat the chicken in it.

Heat the oil in a wok. When hot fry the chicken for about 8 minutes on each side. Add the garlic, ginger, mushrooms, spring onions, stock, wine and soy sauce. Cook for 10 minutes on high heat, stirring occasionally. Stir in the carrots and cabbage. Serve with rice.

Tip: Try this with pork fillet or for a variation, slice the chicken breast into strips before dipping into batter and deep-frying.

Cheesy Chicken

Serves: 4
Prep: 10 mins
Cook: 1 hour

For a really economical dinner party idea you simply can't beat this smashing recipe from Jane Lindsay of Reading in Berkshire.

4 chicken breasts, skinned and boned

2 oz/50 g seasoned flour

4 oz/125 g Cambazola cheese

4 slices unsmoked back bacon

1 tsp/5 ml dried mixed herbs

14 oz/396 g can tomatoes, chopped

4 fl oz/100 ml dry white wine

2 avocado pears

juice one lemon

Preheat the oven to Gas Mark 4/350F/180C.

Coat the chicken with seasoned flour. Cut the cheese into four, place a piece of cheese on each breast and roll up tightly. Wrap round with a piece of bacon and secure with a cocktail stick. Place in a shallow ovenproof dish.

Put the herbs, tomatoes and wine in a saucepan, bring to the boil and simmer for 5 minutes. Pour over the chicken and cook in the oven for about 50 minutes. Peel the avocado, remove the stone and thinly slice. Sprinkle it with lemon juice and place on top of the chicken. Cook for a further 10 minutes.

Serve with new potatoes, courgettes and buttered carrots or with fresh pasta and crisp green side salad.

Cakes
and Puddings

Austrian Apple and Meringue Flan

Serves: 6
Prep: 15 mins plus
30 mins chilling
Cook: 45 mins

4 oz/125 g plain flour

1 oz/25 g icing sugar

1 oz/25 g ground almonds

2½ oz/65 g butter, softened

3 tsp/15 ml chilled milk

filling:

3 eggs, separated

1 lb/450 g cooking apples, stewed

6 oz/175 g caster sugar

2 oz/50 g ground almonds

This continental style flan is at its very best served hot with cream or ice-cream. Created by Mavis Priestley, Hipperholme, West Yorks.

Preheat the oven to Gas Mark 6/400F/200C.

First make the pastry. Place half the flour with the sugar, butter and milk in a medium size bowl and beat together. Mix in the remaining flour and ground almonds to form a firm dough. Wrap in cling film and chill for half an hour. Roll the pastry out on a floured surface and line an 8 in/20 cm flan dish and bake blind for 15 minutes.

For the filling, beat the egg yolks into the stewed apples and spoon into the pastry base. Top with ground almonds.

Whisk the egg whites until they form soft peaks, then gradually fold in caster sugar until stiff. Spoon on top of the apple and ground almond mixture and peak up the meringue. Reduce the oven temperature to Gas Mark 2/300F/150C and bake for half an hour until crisp and set. Serve hot with ice-cream or cream.

Paradise Dessert

Serves: 4–6
Prep: 10 mins
Cook: 2 mins

Pauline Rifkind from Pinner in Middlesex describes her favourite dessert as a dinner party must. After tasting it we tend to agree!

mousse:

3 eggs, separated

1 oz/25 g castor sugar

6 oz/175 g chocolate, plain

syllabub:

4–5 tbsp/60–70 ml advocat

2 tbsp/30 ml ginger marmalade

½ pint/300 ml double cream, whipped

Beat the egg yolks and sugar until pale and creamy. Melt the chocolate with 3 tbsp/45 ml water over a pan of hot water. Mix the warm chocolate with egg yolk mixture. Whisk the egg whites until stiff and fold into the chocolate mix.

Make the syllabub by beating together the advocat and marmalade and fold into whipped cream.

Spoon alternate amounts of mousse and syllabub into large wine glasses. Chill for at least 3 hours. Decorate with frosted grapes.

Tip: To make frosted grapes, brush grapes with egg white and dip in caster sugar. Always use very fresh eggs when using them raw and store them in a fridge.

Over the page, clockwise from left: Hazelnut and Raspberry Meringue, Paradise Dessert, Pears in Red Wine, Austrian Apple and Meringue Flan, Whisky Ginger Cream and Chestnut and Almond Delight

Whisky Ginger Cream

Serves: 4
Prep: 10 mins
Cook: No cook

A great dinner party favourite. Men seem to particularly enjoy this one! From Mrs O. Trippier of Rayton.

2 tbsp/30 ml whisky

2 tbsp/30 ml ginger marmalade

2 tbsp/30 ml caster sugar

grated rind of lemon

½ pint/10 fl oz/284 ml double cream, chilled

2 egg whites

1 kiwi fruit

Mix together the whisky, marmalade, sugar and lemon rind in a bowl, and leave to stand for 15 minutes. Stir the cream into the whisky mixture until evenly blended then whisk with an electric hand whisk or balloon whisk until thick. Beat the egg whites until stiff, then fold into the cream mixture. Spoon into 4 individual wine or sundae glasses. Chill in the fridge for at least 30 minutes.

Decorate with kiwi fruit or fruit of your choice. Serve with Langues de Chat or Brandy Snaps.

Irish Coffee Creams

Serves: 4
Prep: 20 mins
Cook: No cook

Definitely a dinner party special, this one from Mrs E. Mitchell of Budleigh Salterton, Devon. Dark, sophisticated and very, very rich.

4 trifle sponges

8 tbsp/120 ml strong black coffee

½ pint/10 fl oz/284 ml carton double cream

4 tbsp/60 ml Irish Cream Liqueur

2 chocolate flake bars

Break up the trifle sponges and divide between 4 dessert glasses or large wine glasses. Pour 2 tbsp/30 ml black coffee into each glass and leave to soak into the sponge. Meanwhile, whisk together the double cream and the Irish Cream liqueur until the mixture is thick but not too stiff. Divide this mixture between the 4 glasses and top each with half a chocolate flake bar, crumbled. Chill before serving.

Hazelnut and Raspberry Meringue

Serves: 4–6
Prep: 25 mins
Cook: 30–40 mins

Jean McKay from Kirkcaldy, Fife, sent us this recipe. 'Hazelnut Meringue makes a special sweet but I like it best as a cake for a teatime treat!'

4 egg whites

9 oz/250 g caster sugar

few drops of vanilla essence

½ tsp/2.5 ml vinegar

4 oz/125 g toasted ground hazelnuts

½ pint/10 fl oz/284 ml carton double cream, whipped

8 oz/225 g raspberries

1 tbsp/15 ml icing sugar

Preheat the oven to Gas Mark 3/325F/160C.

Grease 2 × 8 in/20 cm sandwich tins and line with baking parchment.

Whisk the egg whites in a grease-free bowl with an electric hand whisk until stiff, then whisk in the caster sugar tablespoonful by tablespoonful until mixture is very stiff. Stir in vanilla essence and vinegar. Fold in the hazelnuts. Divide the mixture between the two prepared tins. Bake for 30–40 minutes. Allow to cool in tins, before removing. Carefully peel off base paper. Sandwich together with whipped cream and raspberries. Pipe rosettes of cream round edge, topping each with a raspberry. Dust with icing sugar.

Tip: To make vanilla sugar, place a vanilla pod in a jar of caster sugar and leave for at least 1 week. Frozen raspberries can be used when fresh are out of season.

Pineapple Ice Cream in Ginger Baskets

This exam-winning recipe sent in by Miss M. C. Hood from South Shields, Tyne and Wear, was just as successful with our judges.

Serves: 4
Prep: 20 mins plus
27 hours freezing
Cook: 7–10 mins

ice-cream:

1 lb/454 g can pineapple, drained

1 egg yolk

1 oz/25 g caster sugar

¼ pint/5 fl oz/142 ml carton single cream

¼ pint/5 fl oz/142 ml carton double cream

1–2 tbsp/15–30 ml crystallised ginger to garnish

ginger baskets:

1 oz/25 g butter

1 oz/25 g caster sugar

1 tbsp/15 ml golden syrup

1 oz/25 g plain flour

¼ tsp/1.25 ml ground ginger

crystallised ginger, to decorate

To make the ice-cream, blend or process the fruit to a smooth purée. Beat the egg yolk and sugar together until creamy. Warm the single cream in a pan, pour on to the egg mixture and stir thoroughly until combined. Set the bowl over a pan of simmering water and stir until the mixture thickens enough to coat the back of a spoon. Cool. Lightly whip the double cream and fold into the custard with the fruit purée. Transfer the mixture to a freezer container and place in the freezer for about 3 hours.

Remove from freezer. Transfer to a large bowl and with an electric hand whisk break down the ice crystals. Return to the freezer for further 24 hours.

To make the baskets, preheat the oven to Gas Mark 4/350F/180C. Place the butter, sugar and syrup in a heavy based pan, and heat until sugar is dissolved. Stir in the flour and the ginger. Spoon 3 or 4 teaspoonfuls of the mixture on to a greased baking sheet, spaced about 3 in/7.5 cm apart. Flatten each ball slightly. Bake for 7–10 minutes until bubbly and a golden colour.

Allow to cool slightly for about 30 seconds to 1 minute. Have four oranges, cups or ramekins ready. With a palette knife lift one at a time and quickly and carefully mould over the upturned cup and shape into a basket. Repeat with any remaining mixture. Remove baskets from cups when cold.

To serve, soften the ice-cream in the fridge for 5–10 minutes. Using a small ice cream scoop or teaspoon place 2–3 balls in each basket. Decorate with crystallised ginger.

Pears in Red Wine Syrup

Serves: 4
Prep: 10 mins plus overnight soaking
Cook: 30 mins

Another really unique recipe from the Daventry William Parker School, Northants. This one by Adam Nicholson – well done!

2 oz/50 g sugar

½ pint/300 ml red wine

8 pears, peeled, cored and halved

1 cinnamon stick

Dissolve the sugar in the red wine with ½ pint/300 ml water. Add the pears and cinnamon stick and simmer for half an hour. Cover and leave overnight.

To serve, place a large oval of ice-cream on a plate and place pears around ice-cream, then pour over the syrup.

Tip: Other drinks can be used – try ginger wine and cider, white wine with a little Cointreau, or even apple or orange juice.

Chestnut and Almond Delight

Serves: 4
Prep: 10 mins
Cook: No cook

2½ oz/65 g unsalted butter

8 oz/226 g can chestnut purée

2 tsp/10 ml Amaretto

2 oz/50 g blanched almonds, toasted

4 chocolate cases

8 fl oz/227 ml carton clotted cream

4 chocolate leaves or buttons to decorate

'Although it looks quite small, don't be tempted to serve more. This is a very rich dessert.'
Created by Mrs Julia Alexander Gordon from Reading in Berkshire.

Cream together the butter and the chestnut purée until thoroughly blended. Mix in the Amaretto and almonds, keeping four aside. Beat together. Chill for 1 hour or so.

Put a spoonful of the mixture on one side of the chocolate case and a spoonful of clotted cream on the other. Top with a toasted almond and chocolate leaf.

Tip: Chocolate cases are available from supermarkets. To make your own, brush several layers of good-quality melted chocolate around paper cakecases and allow to set before peeling off.

Baked Vanilla Cheesecake

Serves: 6
Prep: 20 mins
Cook: 40 mins

A really economical cheesecake with a creamy vanilla topping. From Xanthe Wynne-Jones, West Hampstead, London.

3 oz/75 g butter, melted

6 oz/175 g digestive biscuits, crushed

1½ oz/40 g caster sugar

filling:

6 oz/175 g curd cheese

1 egg

2 oz/50 g caster sugar

½ tsp/2.5 ml vanilla essence

½ tsp/2.5 ml lemon juice

topping:

½ pint/10 fl oz/284 ml carton sour cream

1 oz/25 g caster sugar

¼ tsp/1.5 ml vanilla essence

Preheat the oven to Gas Mark 4/350F/180C.

Lightly grease an 8 in/20 cm spring-form tin. To make the base add the butter and sugar to the crushed biscuits, mix well and press into prepared tin.

Next, prepare the filling. Beat the cheese with the egg, sugar, vanilla essence and lemon juice. Pour on to the base and bake for 30 minutes. Cool for 5 minutes. Reduce oven temperature to Gas Mark 3/325F/160C.

Meanwhile mix the sugar with sour cream and vanilla essence and pour the topping over cheesecake. Bake for a further 10 minutes and leave to cool. Chill before serving.

Serve with a topping or either piped cream, raspberries, blackcurrants, or strawberries or grated chocolate.

Tip: This cake freezes well.

White Chocolate Mousse with Raspberry Coulis

Serves: 4
Prep: 5 mins plus 4 hours chilling time
Cook: 5 mins

A dessert that looks tricky to make but Natalie Varle from Fulham in London makes it easy for you.

6 oz/175 g white chocolate, grated or use buttons

6 tbsp/90 ml warm milk

2 tsp/10 ml gelatine, dissolved in water

2 egg whites

2 drops lemon juice

pinch salt

8 fl oz/227 ml carton whipping cream, whipped

raspberry coulis:

8 oz/225 g raspberries

sugar, to taste

to decorate:

fresh raspberries

mint leaves

Place the chocolate and milk in a bowl over a pan of simmering, not *boiling* water. Heat until melted. Cool the mixture. Fold in the dissolved gelatine.

Whisk the egg whites with lemon juice and salt until thick. Fold into chocolate mixture with the whipped cream. Spoon into four ramekin dishes. Chill for at least 4 hours. To make the raspberry coulis, blend the raspberries and sugar together in a blender or food processor until smooth. Pass through sieve to remove pips.

To serve, unmould the mousse on to individual plates. Surround with raspberry coulis and garnish with fresh raspberries, mint leaves and sieved icing sugar.

Baked Vanilla Cheesecake, White Chocolate Mousse with Raspberry Coulis, Pineapple Icecream in Ginger Basket and Irish Coffee Creams

Chocolate Fudge Pudding

Serves: 4
Prep: 15 mins
Cook: 40 mins

4 oz/125g butter or margarine

4 oz/125 g caster sugar

2 eggs, beaten

2 tbsp/30 ml cocoa

3 oz/75 g self raising flour

pinch salt

½ tsp/2.5 ml vanilla essence

2–3 tbsp/30–45 ml milk

sauce:

2 tbsp/30 ml cocoa

4 oz/125 g soft brown sugar

As Pippa White from Burley in Leeds says, 'This pudding is a kids' delight. The chocolate sauce soaks through the sponge making it a lovely "fudge" underneath.'

Preheat the oven to Gas Mark 5/375F/190C.

Grease a 2 pint/1.2 litre soufflé dish. Cream the butter and sugar until light and fluffy. Gradually add the beaten egg. Sieve the cocoa, flour and salt and fold into the mixture. Mix in the vanilla essence and a little milk to make a soft dropping consistency. Spoon into dish.

Make the sauce by dissolving the cocoa and brown sugar in ½ pint/300 ml boiling water. Pour the sauce over the sponge mixture and bake for 40 minutes until well risen. The sauce soaks down into the sponge leaving a well risen sponge with a fudgy chocolate sauce underneath.

Variations:
Replace hot water in sauce with strong black coffee, or for special occasions replace 2 tbsp/30 ml coffee with Tia Maria. Add chopped nuts, almonds, walnuts or hazelnuts to sauce.

Microwave tip:
Make as above and microwave on high for 7 minutes.

Orange and Lemon Pudding

Serves: 4–6
Prep: 20 mins
Cook: 30–45 mins

2 oz/50 g butter

4 oz/125 g caster sugar

2 eggs, separated

1 oz/25 g plain flour

1 oz/25 g ground almonds

juice of 1½ lemons

juice of 1½ oranges

½ pint/300 ml milk

Tiny, soufflé style puddings that are equally delicious hot or cold. From Jennifer Faulkner, from Dorking in Surrey.

Preheat the oven to Gas Mark 4/350F/180C.

Cream together the butter and sugar until light and fluffy. Beat in the egg yolks, flour, almonds, juice and milk. Whisk the egg whites until stiff, then fold in the rest of the mixture. Spoon into a buttered 2 pint/1.2 litre ovenproof dish and bake for 45 minutes, or into 8 buttered ramekin dishes and bake for 30 minutes, in a bain-marie. Serve hot or cold.

Tip: For a bain-marie, place dish in a roasting pan and half fill pan with water. This stops the mixture from curdling and helps it to set.

1930 Carrot Pudding, Chocolate Fudge Pudding and Orange and Lemon Pudding

1930 Carrot Pudding

Makes: 2
Prep: 10 mins
Cook: 6 hours
plus 3 hours
reheating

8 oz/225 g carrots, peeled and grated

8 oz/225 g mashed potatoes

8 oz/225 g brown breadcrumbs

8 oz/225 g suet

8 oz/225 g brown sugar

2 oz/50 g mixed peel, chopped

8 oz/225 g currants

8 oz/225 g raisins

pinch salt

1 tsp/5 ml baking powder

4 fl oz/100 ml rum or brandy

brandy butter:

4 oz/125 g butter, unsalted

1 tbsp/15 ml caster sugar

1 tbsp/15 ml brandy

Dores Hawks of Framlingham, Suffolk, may have included some unusual ingredients in her dessert but they make a beautifully light and tasty pudding.

Mix together all the ingredients and divide between two 1½ pint/1 litre pudding basins. Place a double sheet of greaseproof paper and foil over each basin and secure with foil. Steam for 6 hours the first day. Reheat and steam for 3 hours when required.

Serve with brandy butter. To make the butter, cream all the ingredients together until light and fluffy.

Peach and Orange Sorbet

Serves: 4–6
Prep: 20 mins plus
overnight soaking
Cook: 30 mins

A refreshing and flavoursome dessert that looks wonderfully elegant served in sparkling wine goblets, from David Symons, Exeter.

3 dried peaches

3 camomile tea bags

1 large orange

8 oz/225 g granulated sugar

1 tbsp/15 ml calvados or brandy

Place the dried peaches and camomile bags in a bowl and cover with 1½ pints/900 ml boiling water. Leave to soak overnight.

Peel the orange, remove the pith, membranes and pips, roughly chop and stir into the soaked peaches with the sugar. Pour the mixture into the saucepan, bring to the boil, cover and simmer for 30 minutes. Allow to cool until tepid. Remove the teabags, add the calvados, pour into a liquidiser or processor and liquidise thoroughly. Pour into a freezer-proof container and cool completely. Switch freezer to fast-freeze, place container in freezer and stir occasionally to break up ice crystals and produce a snow-textured frozen mixture. This will take a couple of hours. Remove from freezer half an hour before serving. Serve in chilled wine goblets decorated with a sprig of mint.

Bread Pudding

Serves: 6–8
Prep: 5 mins
Cook: 1–1¼ hours

12 oz/350 g brown or white breadcrumbs

¾ pint/450 ml milk

7 oz/200 g currants

2 oz/50 g mixed peel

9 oz/250 g sultanas or raisins

5 oz/150 g soft margarine

6 oz/175 g demerara sugar

4 tsp/60 ml mixed spice

2 eggs, beaten

nutmeg

caster sugar

Everyone has a favourite bread pudding recipe. This one is from Karen Rowe of Wantage in Oxfordshire. We think it's smashing.

Preheat the oven to Gas Mark 4/350F/180C.

Soak the breadcrumbs in the milk for about 15 minutes. Beat in the remaining ingredients except the nutmeg and caster sugar. Grease a 2 pint/1.2 litre ovenproof dish. Pour the mixture into the dish. Cook for about 1–1¼ hours until firm and golden. Remove from oven, dredge with caster sugar and nutmeg. Cool and cut into 6–8 portions.

Tip: Bread Pudding can be frozen in portions, defrosted for a few hours and reheated for 5 minutes.

Bread Pudding, Nutty Apples and Country Apple Pud

Nutty Apples

Serves: 4
Prep: 40 mins
Cook: 30–45 mins

Thérèse Brook from Bognor Regis in Sussex found this recipe written on a card inside a jumble sale cookery book. Definitely an up-market apple!

4 small cooking apples, peeled and cored

1 egg, separated

2 oz/50 g digestive biscuits, crushed

2 oz/50 g soft brown sugar

2 oz/50 g almonds or mixed nuts, chopped

4 oz/125 g marzipan

Preheat the oven to Gas Mark 4/350F/180C.

Brush each apple with beaten egg white. Mix the biscuits, sugar and nuts together then roll each apple in the mixture. Place in a baking dish.

Roll out the marzipan on a floured surface and cut out eight leaves, two for each apple.

Knead the egg yolk into the remaining biscuit mixture and fill the centre of each apple with some of this. Bake in oven for 30 minutes until golden. Serve with cream or custard.

Tip: For an extra-special treat, add a dash of brandy to the soft brown sugar.

Profiteroles with Banana Cream

Serves: 4–6
Prep: 20 mins
Cook: 15 mins

choux pastry:

2½ oz/65 g plain flour

½ tsp/2.5 ml salt

2 oz/50 g butter, cut into small pieces

2 eggs, well beaten

filling:

¼ pint/5 fl oz/142 ml carton double cream

large banana, mashed

1 tbsp/15 ml icing sugar

1 tbsp/15 ml Tia Maria (optional)

sauce:

2 Mars bars

2 tbsp/30 ml milk

Simply the most sensational profiteroles you will have ever tasted. A clever idea from Angie Anthony of St Martin, Jersey.

Preheat the oven to Gas Mark 7/425F/220C.

To make the choux pastry, sift the flour and salt on to a piece of greaseproof paper.

Heat the butter and ¼ pint/150 ml cold water in a pan. When the butter has melted, bring to the boil. Remove from heat immediately and tip in the flour. Beat well with a wooden spoon until the paste is smooth and a ball forms leaving the sides of the pan clean. Return to heat and cook for 1 minute. Remove from heat and allow to cool a little, then gradually beat in the eggs until the mixture resembles a stiff paste. Place spoonfuls of the mixture the size of a large walnut on to 2 greased baking sheets. Cook immediately for 15–20 minutes until light and golden brown. Pierce the sides of each choux bun with a sharp pointed knife to let the steam out. Return to oven for a further minute. Place buns on wire tray and allow to cool. (They can be frozen at this stage).

Make the filling for the buns one hour before you want to serve the dessert. Whip the cream until just thick, fold in the bananas, icing sugar and Tia Maria, if using. Place a teaspoonful of the mixture into each bun, place on a glass plate or cake stand and pile high like a pyramid. Place the Mars bars in a bowl with milk or brandy, and melt over a pan of water. Remove, beat with a fork and pour over profiteroles.

Tip: Melt Mars bar in a microwave on high for 1 minute.

Country Apple Pud

Serves: 4–6
Prep: 15 mins
Cook: 20–25 mins

3 large cooking apples
2 tbsp/30 ml white sugar
1 oz/25 g margarine
2 oz/50 g oats
1 oz/25 g brown sugar
2 oz/50 g sultanas
1 oz/25 g currants
1 oz/25 g raisins
1 oz/25 g chopped nuts
1 tsp/5 ml cinnamon
whipped cream, to serve

Laura Hand from Melbourne, Derbyshire, has created a baked apple pudding that tastes divine. Served with cream it's even better!

Preheat the oven to Gas Mark 5/375F/190C. Grease a 7 in/18 cm square baking pan.

Peel, core and slice the apple. Place in a saucepan with the white sugar and 1 tbsp/15 ml water. Cook for 5–10 minutes until just soft.

Meanwhile melt the margarine, remove from heat and add the oats, brown sugar and lemon juice. Drain the apples and add to oats with remaining ingredients. Mix well. Spoon into the prepared tin and bake for 20 minutes until firm to touch. Serve hot or cold with whipped cream.

Microwave tip:
Cook the apple on high in the microwave for 2–3 minutes. Melt the margarine on high for 1 minute. Spoon into a prepared dish and microwave on high for 7 minutes.

Over the page, clockwise from top left: Cherriots of Fire, Profiteroles with Banana Cream, Meringue Slice, Peach and Orange Sorbet and Caramelised Raspberry Dessert

Caramelised Raspberry Dessert

Serves: 4–6
Prep: 5 mins
Cook: 5 mins

1 lb/450 g fresh raspberries

1 tbsp/15 ml crème de cassis or raspberry liqueur

12 oz/350 g cream cheese

¼ pint/5 fl oz/142 ml carton double cream

2 oz/50 g icing sugar

3–4 oz/75–125 g caster sugar

The raspberry season is a short one, so make the most of this gorgeous flavour with this unusual dessert from Fiona Ambroziak of Westerham, Kent.

Place the raspberries in the base of shallow heat-proof dish. Sprinkle over the liqueur.

Beat the cream cheese, cream and icing sugar together until smooth. Spread the cheese mixture over raspberries. Sprinkle liberally with caster sugar making sure the whole surface is covered.

Place under a pre-heated grill and cook for a couple of minutes until surface bubbles and turns golden brown. Chill before serving. Serve on its own or with more raspberries.

Tip: Apricots, peaches and blackcurrants are just as delicious used in this recipe.

Meringue Slice

Serves: 10
Prep: 20 mins
Cook: 40 mins

7 oz/200 g stoned dates

8 oz/225 g sponge fingers

7 oz/200 g walnuts

1 tsp/5 ml baking powder

8 egg whites

14 oz/400 g caster sugar

to decorate:

½ pint/10 fl oz/284 ml carton double cream

¼ pint/5 fl oz/142 ml carton single cream

mint leaves, frosted fruit to garnish

Fiona Ross from By Banchory, Kincardineshire, sent in this recipe. 'It's my favourite and makes a sensational Special Occasion dessert.'

Preheat the oven to Gas Mark 3/325F/160C.

Grease and line an 8 in/20 cm × 12 in/30 cm Swiss roll tin. Chop the dates, sponge fingers and walnuts into ½ in/1.5 cm pieces. Mix together in a large bowl with the baking powder.

Whisk the egg whites until stiff. Fold in the sugar and whisk until the mixture is thick and stiff. Fold the egg whites into date mixture. Spoon into prepared tin. Bake in oven for 40 minutes until lightly browned. Leave in the tin until cool.

Carefully slide out on to a board. Peel away the paper and cut in half lengthways. Slide one half on to a long serving plate. Spread half the whipped cream on to the meringue base and top with second meringue slice. Spread remaining cream on top and decorate.

Variation:
Make into a pavlova shape and fill middle with cream.

Cherriots of Fire

Serves: 3–4
Prep: 5 mins
Cook: 10 mins

14 oz/396 g can black cherries, stoned

juice and zest of 1 orange

1 oz/25 g crystallised or stem ginger, chopped

1 tsp/5 ml cornflour, blended with 1 tbsp/15 ml water

2 tbsp/30 ml brandy

A clever mix of flavours that add up to a very different dessert. From Mrs S. Pedelty, West Auckland, County Durham.

Pour the cherries and juice into a frying pan and heat through. Add the orange zest, orange juice and ginger. Stir in cornflour, bring to the boil and thicken. Add brandy to taste. Pour over individual portions of ice-cream and serve with brandy snaps.

Tip: This makes a delicious filling for pancakes.

Swiss Truffle Cake

Serves: 6–8
Prep: 10 mins
Cook: 35–40 mins

Vérène Hull-Grieshaber from London remembers her grandmother making this cake. 'Its rather strange looks hide a very rich intense flavour. It's loved by everyone, especially children.'

9 oz/250 g good quality plain chocolate, Suchard Mernier Patissier

4 oz/125 g unsalted butter

4 oz/125 g caster sugar

4 eggs separated

2 tbsp/30 ml plain flour

Preheat the oven to Gas Mark 4/350F/180C. Grease and line an 8 in/20 cm spring-form tin.

Melt the chocolate and butter in a bowl over a saucepan of hot but *not* boiling water. When melted stir in the beaten egg yolks, sugar and flour. Whisk the egg whites until stiff and fold into the chocolate mixture with a large metal spoon. Make sure the mixture is combined well together, being careful not to overbeat. Spoon into prepared tin and cook for 35–40 minutes. The cake is cooked when a skewer comes out wet but not covered in chocolate.

Don't panic when taking it out of the oven – it falls down like a soufflé after half an hour. Leave to chill for 8 hours before removing from tin. Serve the cake with raspberries and vanilla ice-cream and a glass of kirsch and sprinkle with sieved icing sugar.

Variation:
Coffee or vanilla flavour can be added.

Almond Cake

Serves: 4–6
Prep: 10 mins
Cook: 25 mins

4 oz/125 g ground almonds

2 oz/50 g potato flour

5 oz/150 g butter

6 oz/175 g caster sugar

3 eggs, well beaten

This will definitely become a real festive favourite and it's so quick to make! Mrs Mary Godfrey from Sandy, Bedfordshire, created this cake for those with an allergy to wheat. She originally cooked this cake in a microwave.

Preheat the oven to Gas Mark 4/350F/180C. Grease and line a deep 7 in/18 cm cake tin.

Mix together the almonds and potato flour, lifting with a spoon to aerate it.

Cream the butter and sugar together until light and fluffy. Gradually add the beaten egg, a little at a time. Fold in the almonds and potato flour and spoon into prepared tin. Place in the oven for 20–25 minutes, or until firm to touch but still moist. Leave to cool for 10 minutes before turning out on to a wire rack to cool. Serve with sieved icing sugar.

Tip: To cook by microwave, prepare as above then spoon into a prepared microwave dish. Cook on high (700W) for 7–8 minutes and leave to stand for 10 minutes.

This cake freezes very well.

Strawberry Gateau

Serves: 4–6
Prep: 20 mins
Cook: No cook

8 oz/225 g cream cheese

4 tbsp/60 ml caster sugar

grated rind of 1 orange

1 tbsp/15 ml orange liqueur, Cointreau

½ pint/10 fl oz/284 ml carton double cream

18 sponge fingers

2 tbsp/30 ml strawberry jam

8 oz/225 g strawberries, hulled and halved

to garnish:

mint leaves

4 strawberries

A wickedly delicious dessert you couldn't possibly resist. From sixteen-year-old Suzannah Chambers from Stanley Common in Derbyshire.

Grease and line a 2 lb/900 g loaf tin.

Place the cream cheese and sugar in a bowl and whisk together thoroughly until light and fluffy. Whisk in the orange rind, liqueur and double cream until the mixture thickens. Spoon one third of the mixture into the tin and smooth over the surface. Spread the sponge fingers with jam. Cover the mixture in the tin with one layer of sponge fingers, laying lengthwise. Cover the fingers with half the strawberries. Spoon over another third of the cream mixture, repeat the layer of sponge fingers and strawberry halves, finishing with remaining cream mixture. Smooth over the surface and chill for at least 6 hours.

To serve, run a knife around the top edge of the gateau to release it. Invert on to a serving plate. Carefully peel off greaseproof paper. Decorate top with strawberries and mint leaves.

Rich Fruit Cake, Almond Cake, Strawberry Gateau, Swiss Truffle Cake and Blueberry Poppyseed Cake

Blueberry-Poppy Seedcake

Serves: 6–8
Prep: 20 mins
Cook: 1¼ hours

Cindy Long from Orton Malborne, Peterborough, created this very special recipe. She suggests substituting blueberries for strawberries or peaches when they're in season.

6 oz/175 g caster sugar

4 oz/125 g butter or margarine

2 tsp/10 ml lemon rind grated

1 egg, beaten

12 oz/350 g plain flour

2 tbsp/30 ml poppy seeds

½ tsp/2.5 ml bicarbonate of soda

¼ tsp/1.25 ml salt

¼ pint/5 fl oz/142 ml carton soured cream

filling:

8 oz/225g blueberries, fresh or frozen

3 oz/75 g sugar

2 tsp/10 ml flour

¼ tsp/1.25 ml ground nutmeg

glaze:

3 oz/75 g icing sugar

1–2 tbsp/15–30 ml milk

Preheat the oven to Gas Mark 4/350F/180C. Grease and line a 9 in/23 cm spring-form tin.

Cream the butter and sugar together using an electric hand whisk until light and fluffy. Stir in the lemon rind and eggs. Beat for a further 2 minutes.

In a medium size bowl combine the flour, poppy seeds, bicarbonate of soda and salt. Alternately mix into the butter mixture with the soured cream. Dip the back of a spoon in hot water and spread the mixture over bottom of pan and 1 in/2.5 cm up the sides of the cake tin, making sure mixture is at least ¼ in/0.5 cm thick.

Mix the filling ingredients together, then spoon the filling over the mixture in the tin. Bake in oven for approximately 1 hour until crust is golden brown. Cool slightly before removing from tin. Cool on wire rack.

Mix icing sugar and enough milk to form a soft consistency. Drizzle glaze over top of warm cake. Serve warm or cold.

Autumn Bars

Makes: 18 bars
Prep: 10 mins
Cook: 35 mins

6 oz/175 g unsalted butter

6 oz/175 g muscavado sugar

3 oz/75g hazelnuts, chopped

3 oz/75 g dried apples

3 oz/75 g dried pears

3 oz/75 g sultanas

12 oz/350 g wholemeal flour

1 tsp/5 ml allspice

juice of one orange

1 egg, size 3, beaten

1 egg yolk, size 3, beaten

2 tbsp/30 ml clear honey

Rebecca Davies aged fifteen from Pentre Halkyn, Clwyd, makes clever use of dried fruits in her yummy autumn bars.

Preheat the oven to Gas Mark 5/375F/190C and line a shallow 9 in/25 cm square tin.

Place the butter and sugar in a heavy pan and dissolve the sugar over a low heat. Chop the dried fruits and nuts and add to a large bowl with the flour and spice. Reserve a small amount of each for the topping.

Make a well in the centre of the flour and stir in the egg, egg yolk, orange juice and the dissolved butter and sugar. Stir well until well combined and spoon into the tin. Bake in oven for about 35 mins. Remove from the oven and cool in the tin for 5 minutes.

Turn out on to a board and cut into 18 slices with a sharp knife. Warm the honey and brush on the tops of the bars. Sprinkle over the remaining dried fruits and hazelnuts and leave for about 10 mins. Serve.

Tip: Any fruits can be used but they must be dried as fresh fruit will shrivel when baked and will go bad if not eaten within a few days as the topping. Other sweet spices can be substituted for the allspice, such as nutmeg, cinnamon.

Date Slices

Makes: 16
Prep: 20 mins
Cook: 25 mins

Definitely more-ish. These scrummy slices are the kind of small cakes that sell well at fêtes and bazaars. From Janice Catchpole, Wisbech, Cambridgeshire.

8 oz/225 g packet sugar-rolled chopped dates

grated rind and juice of half a lemon

6 oz/175 g margarine

4 oz/125 g sugar

6 oz/175 g self raising flour

6 oz/175 g rolled porridge oats

1 tsp/5 ml bicarbonate of soda

Preheat the oven to Gas Mark 4/350F/180C.

Grease a 7 in/18 cm × 11 in/28 cm tin.

Place the dates in a saucepan with ¼ pint/150 ml water, lemon rind and juice. Bring to the boil and simmer gently until the dates become soft and pulpy.

Cream margarine with sugar until light and fluffy. Gradually mix in the flour and porridge oats. Add the bicarbonate of soda. Spread half the mixture into the baking tin. Press firmly to form a layer. Spread with cooled date mixture. Spread remaining mixture evenly over dates. Press gently. Bake for 25 minutes until golden brown.

Cut into slices when cold. Can be served as a teatime treat or with custard as a pudding.

Date Slices, Caribbean Cookies, Autumn Bars and Marigold Shortbread

Caribbean Cookies

Makes: 15 biscuits
Prep: 10 mins
Cook: 10–15 mins

Quick, simple and delicious, these biscuits are guaranteed to disappear fast! From R. C. Tecwyn, Rhosgadfan, Gwynedd.

4 oz/125 g self-raising wholemeal flour

1 oz/25g desiccated coconut

2 oz/50 g sugar

grated rind of 1 orange

4 oz/125 g margarine

Preheat the oven to Gas Mark 4/350F/180C and grease a baking sheet. Place the dry ingredients into a bowl. Stir in the orange rind. Rub in the margarine, using fingertips, and knead together to form a dough. Form into small balls and place on to the baking sheet. Flatten the surface with a fork. Bake in oven for 10–15 minutes until golden. Cool on a wire rack.

Marigold Shortbread

Serves: 4–6
Prep: 15 mins
Cook: 25 mins

The prettiest shortbread you'll ever see and it tastes great too. Mrs E. Solesbury from Staunton, Gloucestershire, is the creator of this recipe.

4 oz/125g butter

2 oz/50 g caster sugar

6 oz/175 g plain flour

1 oz/25g ground almonds

1 tsp/5 ml apple mint, chopped

1 tbsp/15 ml marigold petals

Preheat the oven to Gas Mark 6/400F/200C. Grease a 7 in/18 cm sandwich tin.

Cream the butter and sugar together until fluffy, then stir in flour and ground almonds a little at a time. Mix in the mint and marigold petals. Knead to form a firm smooth dough. Press into a prepared tin and cook for about 25 minutes until golden. Mark into 6–8 pieces while hot. Dredge with caster sugar and remove from tin when cold.

Apple and Sultana Cake

Serves: 4–6
Prep: 20 mins
Cook: 1½–1¾ hours

8 oz/225 g cooking apples

8 oz/225 g sultanas

¼ pint/150 ml milk

6 oz/175 g sugar

12 oz/350 g self-raising flour

2 tsp/10 ml mixed spice

6 oz/175 g butter

1 egg, beaten

2 tbsp/30 ml demerara sugar

Mrs C. Kennard from Milton Keynes, Buckinghamshire, says that this moist apple cake works well as a teatime special or makes a filling dessert with lashings of custard.

Preheat the oven to Gas Mark 3/325F/160C. Grease and line a deep square 8 in/20 cm cake tin.

Peel, core and cut the apple into small pieces and place in a large bowl with the sultanas, milk and sugar.

In a separate bowl sieve the flour and spice together, rub the butter into the flour to resemble breadcrumbs, then stir into the fruit mixture with the egg. Mix well. When combined, spoon into prepared tin. Sprinkle the demerara sugar over the top and bake for 1½–1¾ hours until well-risen and golden. Leave to cool on a wire rack. Serve warm with custard as a pud or as a cake for tea.

Tip: This cake keeps for several days if kept wrapped and covered.

Raisin Loaf

Makes: 2 lb/900 g loaf tin
Prep: 15 mins
Cook: 50 mins

'As my family adore raisins and home made bread I combined the two in this easy to make tea loaf,' says Mrs A. E. Nawell of Henley-on-Thames, Oxfordshire.

2 oz/50 g margarine

8 oz/225 g sugar

1 egg, beaten

1 lb/450 g strong flour

8 oz/225 g raisins

1 tsp/5 ml vanilla essence

1 tsp/5 ml cinnamon

1½ tsp/7.5 ml nutmeg

1 tbsp/15 ml baking powder

½ tsp/2.5 ml bicarbonate soda

½ tsp/2.5 ml salt

8 fl oz/250 ml sour milk

Preheat the oven to Gas Mark 4/350F/180C. Grease and line a 2 lb/900 g loaf tin.

Cream the margarine and sugar together until fluffy. Gradually beat in the egg and vanilla.

Coat the raisins in 1 tbsp/15 ml flour and warm through in oven.

Meanwhile sieve the remaining dry ingredients and add a little at a time to the creamed mixture with the sour milk. Mix in the raisins, spoon into prepared tin and cook in oven for 50 minutes until golden and well-risen. Cool on a wire rack. Serve warm or cold.

Tip: To sour milk, add 1 tbsp/15 ml lemon juice to milk or use soured cream for a richer texture.

Over the page, clockwise from top left: Apricot Fruit Cake, Raisin Loaf, Banana Bread, Apple and Sultana Cake, Golden Cake and Creamy Topped-Carrot Cake

Banana Bread

Makes: 1 lb/450 g
Prep: 15 mins
Cook: 1 hour

Daventry William Parker School, Northants, have come up trumps yet again! This time it's moist and delicious tea bread from Rebecca Whitbread aged just eleven years.

4 oz/125 g margarine

4 oz/125 g sugar

2 large ripe bananas, mashed

½ tsp/2.5 ml baking soda

½ tsp/2.5 ml salt

12 oz/350 g self-raising flour

4 oz/125 g sultanas

a little milk

Preheat the oven to Gas Mark 3/325F/160C. Grease and line a 1 lb/450 g loaf tin.

Cream the margarine and sugar until light and fluffy. Mix in the bananas, sieve the baking soda, salt and flour and stir into the creamed mixture. Mix in the sultanas and enough milk to make a soft but not runny consistency. Spoon into the prepared tin and smooth top. Bake in the centre of oven for 1 hour, cut in slices and serve with butter.

Variation:
Replace sultanas with chopped walnuts.

Tip: This cake freezes very well. Defrost at room temperature for a couple of hours.

Creamy Topped Carrot Cake

Serves: 8
Prep: 12 mins
Cook: 55 mins

4 oz/125 g margarine

3 oz/75 g soft brown sugar

2 eggs beaten

4 oz/125 g self raising flour

1 tsp/5 ml baking powder

1 tsp/5 ml salt

1 tsp/5 ml vanilla essence

1 tsp/5 ml cinnamon

4 oz/125 g carrots, grated

2 oz/50 g crushed pineapple, drained

2 oz/50 g walnuts, chopped

topping:

4 oz/125 g cream cheese

4 oz/125 g icing sugar

1 tbsp/15 ml single cream

rind of one orange

This is certainly a fast cake – the whole lot is mixed at speed in a food processor. From D. Evans, Newport, Gwent.

Preheat the oven to Gas Mark 4/350F/180C. Line and grease a 1 lb/450 g loaf tin.

In a large bowl cream together the margarine and brown sugar until pale and fluffy. Gradually beat in the eggs then stir in the flour, baking powder, salt, vanilla essence and cinnamon until well mixed. Add the remaining ingredients and mix well. Pour the mixture into the prepared tin and flatten centre to allow for rising. Bake for 55 minutes or until skewer comes out clean, then allow to cool. For the topping, cream together the cheese and sugar then add the cream and grated orange rind. Cover the top of the cake with the mixture and fork top and leave to set.

Tip: This cake freezes very well. Defrost at room temperature for a few hours before serving.

Apricot Fruit Cake

Serves: 6–8
Prep: 15 mins
Cook: 1¾–2 hours

Mrs Sheila Johnson of Stanley, County Durham, makes this healthy cake for birthdays, Christmas- and Easter-time.

4 oz/125 g glacé cherries, halved

4 oz/125 g dried apricots, chopped

1 lb/450 g mixed fruit

5 oz/150 g butter or margarine

6 fl oz/175 ml red wine

6 oz/175 g golden syrup

2 oz/50 g chopped nuts (optional)

8 oz/225 g granary flour

1 tsp/5 ml mixed spice

½ tsp/1.25 ml bicarbonate of soda

2 eggs, beaten

Preheat the oven to Gas Mark 2/300F/150C. Grease and line an 8 in/20 cm cake tin.

Place the fruit, butter and wine in a large pan. Bring slowly to the boil and simmer for 5 minutes and cool. Stir in the remaining ingredients, beat well and pour into prepared tin. Bake for 1¾–2 hours. Cool in the tin for 1 hour then cool on wire rack.

This cake can be stored wrapped in foil for up to one week.

Golden Cake

Serves: 12
Prep: 20 mins
Cook: 4 hours

8 oz/225 g dried apricots

14 oz/400 g sultanas

grated rind and juice of two oranges

6 oz/175 g whole almonds

7 oz/200 g golden granulated sugar

7 oz/200 g butter or margarine

1 tbsp/15 ml golden syrup

4 eggs, size 2

8 oz/225 g flour, sieved

6 oz/175 g mixed peel

1 tsp/5 ml ground ginger

1 tsp/5 ml cinnamon

topping:

golden glacé fruit

pineapple, apricots, golden cherries

A rich moist fruitcake that you can ice and decorate for special occasions. From Hilary Wade, Herne Bay, Kent.

Preheat the oven to Gas Mark 2/300F/150C. Line a 9 in/23 cm deep cake tin.

Finely chop the apricots and place in a bowl, add the sultanas, stir in the orange juice and rind. Chop or grind the almond with the skin on, or in a coffee grinder or food processor.

Beat the sugar and butter together until light and fluffy. Add the golden syrup. Gradually beat in the eggs, adding a tablespoonful of flour to prevent curdling. Fold in the sieved flour, add the apricots and sultana mixture, mixed peel, chopped almonds and spices, and mix thoroughly. Spoon the mixture into the cake tin. Make a little hollow in the centre of the cake to ensure it rises evenly. Bake in oven for 3½–4 hours or until a skewer inserted comes out clean. Test every 15 minutes after recommended cooking time. Once cooled, store in greaseproof paper or tin foil. Either decorate with golden glacé fruit or cover with marzipan and ice in the usual way.

Rich Fruit Cake

Serves: 6–8
Prep: 20 mins
Cook: 2–2½ hours

Mrs Moran from Shepperton, Middlesex, could have sent us a book-full of her favourite recipes. This really fruity cake was certainly tempting enough for us to include.

4 oz/125 g raisins

4 oz/125 g sultanas

2 oz/50 g currants

2 oz/50 g glacé cherries, halved

1 oz/25 g chopped mixed peel

1 oz/25 g blanched almonds, chopped

4 oz/125 g dark soft brown sugar

4 oz/125 g butter

6 oz/175 g plain flour

1 oz/25 g cornflour

¼ tsp/1.25 ml salt

1 tsp/5 ml bicarbonate soda

2 tbsp/30 ml sherry

1 tsp/5 ml cocoa

1 tsp/5 ml mixed spice

2 eggs, beaten

½ tsp/2.5 ml almond essence

Preheat the oven to Gas Mark 3/325F/160C. Grease and line a 5½ in/14 cm square or 6 in/15 cm round cake tin.

Mix the fruit and nuts together.

Cream butter and sugar until light and fluffy. Sieve dry ingredients. Dissolve bicarbonate of soda in sherry. Add 1 tbsp/15 ml dry ingredients to creamed mixture, gradually beat in egg mixture. Fold in remaining dry ingredients, soda, sherry, fruit and flavouring. Spoon mixture into cake tin and bake for 2–2½ hours. Reduce oven temperature to Gas Mark 2/300F/150C after first 30 minutes and continue cooking for remaining 1½–2 hours. Cool on a wire rack.

Tip: Marzipan and icing can top this cake for extra-special occasions.

Index

Page numbers in italics indicate illustrations

Aduki Bean Moussaka, *42*, 44
advocat, 97
ale, brown, 58
allspice, 128
almonds, 115
   Almond Cake, 124, *126*
   blanched, 61, 104, 140
   Chestnut and Almond Delight, *98*, 104
   flaked, 48
   ground, 36, 96, 109, 124, 131
   whole, 139
Amaretto, 104
apple
   Apple and Sultana Cake, 132, *134*
   Austrian Apple and Meringue Flan, 96, *99*
   Country Apple Pud, *114*, 117
   dried, 128
   Fillet of Pork Parcels with Apple Rings, 62, *63*
   Mustard and Apple Lamb Chops, 66, *67*
   Nutty Apples, *114*, 115
   Pork 'n' Cider, *67*, 69
   Stilton Stuffed Pork in Pastry, *83*, 89
   stuffing, 34
   Vegetable Curry, *42*, 46
apple mint, 131
apricot, 34, 53, 92, 138, 139
Apricot Fruit Cake, *134*, 138
artichoke
   Savoury Artichoke Spread, *15*, 16
asparagus spears, 61
Aubergines, Stuffed, *42*, 45
Austrian Apple and Meringue Flan, 96, *99*
Autumn Bars, 128, *130*
avocado, 36, 94

bacon, 60
   smoked streaky, 90
   streaky, 58
   unsmoked back, 94
bain-marie, 109
Baked Vanilla Cheesecake, 105, *107*
banana
   Banana Bread, *134*, 136
   Profiteroles with Banana Cream, 116–17, *119*
   Tandoori Chicken with Green Bananas, *50*, 52
beef
   Chilli con Carne, *83*, 84
   Fillet of Pork Parcels with Apple Rings, 62, *63*
   Huntsmans Loaf, 56, *59*
   Spicy Beef and Pepper Hot Pot, 82, *83*
beef stock, 58, 82
beer, 62
   Pork with Beer Sauce, 65, *67*
Benedictine Curried Chicken, *50*, 53
black bean sauce, 75
Blueberry-Poppy Seedcake, *126*, 127
Blushing Smoked Trout Mousse, 12, *15*
Bombay mix, 34
brandy, 14, 25, 53, 88, 111, 112, 122
brandy butter, 111
Bread Pudding, 113, *114*

Brie, 20, 28
broccoli, 41
butter
   brandy, 111
   unsalted, 104, 111, 123, 128

cabbage, 38, 60, 93
calvados, 112
Cambazola cheese, 94
camomile tea, 112
Caramelised Raspberry Dessert, *118*, 120
Caribbean Cookies, *130*, 131
carrot
   Carrot and Coriander Seed Soup, 23, *26*
   Chicken Tropical, 77, *78*
   Creamy Topped Carrot Cake, *134*, 137
   Garlic Chicken, *91*, 93
   glazed, 60
   Mrs M's Mussel Soup, 24, *26*
   1930 Carrot Pudding, *110*, 111
   Tangy Vegetable Au Gratin, 38, *39*
   Vegetable Curry, *42*, 46
casserole
   Pork 'n' Cider, *67*, 69
   Rabbit Casserole, *59*, 60
celery, *46*, 77
cheddar cheese, 28, *30*, 40, 41, 44, 45, 68, 70, 85
cheese
   Cold Chive and Potato Soup with Cheese, *27*, 28
   Crispy Cheese Pancakes with Courgette Sauce, 32–3, *35*
   Savoury Pizzas, 37, *39*
   Spinach and Cheese Soup, 27, *30*
   Stewkey Sea Food Cobbler, *71*, 74
   see also individual types of cheese
cheese sauce, 38, 44
Cheesecake, Baked Vanilla, 105, *107*
Cheesy Chicken, *91*, 94
Cheesy Chicken and Leek, *83*, 85
Cheesy Spirals, *39*, 41
cherries, black
   Cherriots of Fire, *118*, 122
Chestnut and Almond Delight, *98*, 104
chicken
   Benedictine Curried Chicken, *50*, 53
   Cheesy Chicken, *91*, 94
   Cheesy Chicken and Leek, *83*, 85
   Chicken and Pork in Black Bean Sauce, 75, *78*
   Chicken Tropical, 77, *78*
   Fakenham Fricassée, *87*, 92
   Garlic Chicken, *91*, 93
   Herbed Chicken in Coconut Milk, 49, *51*
   Oriental Chicken, 76, *79*
   Shahi Murghi (Royal Chicken), 48, *51*
   Smooth Chicken Paté, 14, *15*
   Tandoori Chicken with Green Bananas, *50*, 52
chicken stock, 25, 28, 29, 30, 53, 57, 66, *77*, 90, 93
Chilli con Carne, *83*, 84

chilli powder, 34, 36, 48, 52, 54, 84
chillies, 49, 52, 54, 82
Chinese leaves, 36
chives
   Cold Chive and Potato Soup with Cheese, *27*, 28
   Garlic and Vermouth Mushrooms, 17, *18*
   Savoury Parsnip Scones, 33, *35*
chocolate
   Chocolate Fudge Pudding, 108, *110*
   Irish Coffee Creams, 100, *107*
   Paradise Dessert, 97, *98*
   Swiss Truffle Cake, 123, *126*
   White Chocolate Mousse with Raspberry Coulis, 106, *107*
chocolate buttons, 106
chocolate cases, 104
chocolate leaves, 104
choux pastry, 117
Cider, Pork 'n', 69
cider vinegar, 81
cinnamon, 36, 40, 103, 116, 133, 137, 139
cloves, ground, 29, 36
cockles, 74
cocoa, 108, 140
coconut, desiccated, 46, 49, 131
Coconut Milk, Herbed Chicken, 49
cod, 72, 74
coffee
   Irish Coffee Creams, 100, *107*
Cointreau, 125
Cold Chive and Potato Soup with Cheese, *27*, 28
coriander
   fresh, 23, 52, 54
   ground, 23, 36, 48, 49, 84
coriander seeds
   Carrot and Coriander Seed Soup, 23, *26*
Country Apple Pud, *114*, 116
courgettes
   Aduki Bean Moussaka, *42*, 44
   Cheesy Spirals, *39*, 41
   Courgette Loaf, *42*, 43
   Crispy Cheese Pancakes with Courgette Sauce, 32–3, *35*
   Petits Pois and Courgette Soup, *27*, 29
crab, 21
cream, 43, 117
   clotted, 104
   double, 53, 56, 88, 97, 100, 101, 102, 116–17, 120, 121, 125
   half-fat, 29
   low-fat, 24
   single, 17, 20, 21, 24, 25, 28, 29, 61, 65, 102, 121, 137
   sour/soured, 12, 105, 127, 133
   whipped/whipping, 106, 116
cream cheese, 13, 120, 125, 137
Creamy Topped Carrot Cake, *134*, 137
crème de cassis, 120
Crispy Cheese Pancakes with Courgette Sauce, 32–3, *35*
cucumber, 20, 86
cumin, ground, 30, 36, 54, 84
currants, 111, 113, 116, 140
curry powder, 21, 38, 46, 53

dates
  Date Slices, 129, *130*
  Meringue Slice, *119*, 121
digestive biscuits, 105, 115
dill, 72, 73
Dolcelatte, 88
Duck, Elizabeth's Raspberry, *55*, 57

Elizabeth's Raspberry Duck, *55*, 57
Exotic Tofu with Melon Salad, *35*, 36

Fakenham Fricassée, *87*, 92
fetta cheese
  Steak with Fetta Salad, 86, *87*
Fillet of Pork Parcels with Apple
  Rings, 62, *63*
filo pastry, 20, 73
fish, white, 21
Fish Cakes, Salmon, 70, *71*
fish stock, 12
five spices powder, 75
Flaky Fish Surprise, *71*, 73
Flan, Austrian Apple and Meringue,
  99, 112
Fresh Melon with Stem Ginger and
  Yoghurt, *18*, 19
fromage frais, 43
frosted fruit, 121

garam masala, 48, 54, 84, 92
garlic
  Garlic and Vermouth Mushrooms,
    17, *18*
  Garlic Chicken, *91*, 93
gelatine, 12, 13, 106
ginger
  crystallised, 102, 107, 122
  fresh, 36, 48, 49, 52, 93
  Fresh Melon with Stem Ginger and
    Yoghurt, *18*, 19
  ground, 54, 76, 77, 80, 139
  Pineapple Ice Cream in Ginger
    Baskets, 102–3, *107*
  root, 81
  stem, 19, 122
glacé fruit, 138, 139, 140
Golden Cake, *135*, 139
golden syrup, 80, 102, 138, 139
grapes, frosted, 97
gravy, 89

haddock, 72, 74
ham, 56, 62, 88
hazelnuts
  Autumn bars, 128, *130*
  Hazelnut and Raspberry
    Meringue, *98*, 101
herb and lemon sauce, 61
honey, 128
Hot Pot, Spicy Beef and Pepper, 82,
  83
Huntsmans Loaf, 56, *59*

ice cream, 107
  Pineapple Ice Cream in Ginger
    Baskets, 102–3, *107*
Irish Coffee Creams, 100, *107*
Irish Cream Liqueur, 100

kidney, 82
kidney beans, 41, 84
kiwi fruit, 100

lamb
  Mustard and Apple Chops, 66, *67*
  Spicy Coated Leg of Lamb, *51*, 54
  Tarragon Lamb Bake, *67*, 68
Lasagne, Seafood, *71*, 72

leeks
  Cheesy Chicken and Leek, *83*, 85
  Leek and Roquefort Soup, 22, *26*
  Tangy Vegetable Au Gratin, 38, *39*
lemon
  grated rind of, 20, 100, 127, 129
  juice, 12, 46, 61, 62, 70, 80, 94, 105,
    106, 109, 129
  Orange and Lemon Pudding, 109,
    110
lemon grass, 49
lentils
  Macaroni and Lentil Bake, *39*, 40
lettuce, 86
lime juice, 48, 49
limes, 36, 48
liver, 62
lobster
  Mock Lobster Soufflé, *18*, 21

Macaroni and Lentil Bake, *39*, 40
Marigold Shortbread, *130*, 131
marjoram, 72
marmalade, ginger, 97, 100
Marrow, Vegetarian Stuffed, 34, *35*
Mars bars, 116–17
martini, 17
marzipan, 115
mayonnaise, 13, 16
Medallions of Veal, *55*, 56
melon
  Exotic Tofu with Melon Salad, *35*, 36
  Fresh Melon with Stem Ginger and
    Yoghurt, *18*, 19
meringue
  Austrian Apple and Meringue
    Flan, *99*, 112
  Hazelnut and Raspberry
    Meringue, *99*, 101
  Meringue Slice, *119*, 121
mint, 19
  apple, 131
mint leaves, 106, 121, 125
Mrs M's Mussel Soup, 24, *26*
mixed herbs, 14, 64, 82, 84, 90, 94
mixed fruit, 138
mixed peel, 111, 113, 139, 140
mixed spice, 113, 132, 138, 140
Mock Lobster Soufflé, *18*, 21
Moussaka, Aduki Bean, *42*, 44
mousse
  Blushing Smoked Trout Mousse,
    12, *15*
  Salmon Mousse, 13, *15*
  White Chocolate Mousse with
    Raspberry Coulis, 106, *107*
Mozzarella cheese, 32
Muscadet, 60
mushrooms
  Aduki Bean Moussaka, *42*, 44
  Chilli con Carne, *83*, 84
  Crispy Cheese Pancakes with
    Courgette Sauce, 32–3, *35*
  Fakenham Fricassée, *87*, 92
  Garlic and Vermouth Mushrooms,
    17, *18*
  Garlic Chicken, *91*, 93
  Huntsmans Loaf, 56, *59*
  Macaroni and Lentil Bake, *39*, 40
  Medallions of Veal, *55*, 56
  Mushroom Bisque, 25, *27*
  Oriental Chicken, 76, *79*
  Seafood Lasagne, *71*, 72
  Speedy Pasta, *87*, 88
  Spicy Beef and Pepper Hot Pot,
    82, *83*
  Stuffed Aubergines, *42*, 45
  Tangy Vegetable Au Gratin, 38, *39*

Taylor Toad Supreme, 64, *67*
Venison Carbonade, 58, *59*
mussels
  Mrs M's Mussel Soup, 24, *26*
mustard
  Mustard and Apple Lamb Chops,
    66, *67*
  Salmon surprise, 61, *62*
  Stewkey Sea Food Cobbler, *71*, 74

nutmeg, 43, 113, 127, 133
nuts
  chopped, 116, 138
  mixed, 115
Nutty Apples, *114*, 115

oats, 116
  porridge, 90, 129
olive oil, 32, 45, 56, 86, 89
olives, black, 86
onions, spring, 13, 53, 70, 81, 93
orange liqueur, 125
oranges
  Autumn Bars, 128, *130*
  Caribbean Cookies, *130*, 131
  Cherriots of Fire, *118*, 122
  Creamy Topped Carrot Cake, *134*,
    137
  Golden Cake, *135*, 139
  Orange and Lemon Pudding, 109,
    110
  Peach and Orange Sorbet, 112, *118*
  Smooth Chicken Paté, 14, *15*
  Strawberry Gateau, 125, *126*
oregano, 40, 44
Oriental Chicken, 76, *79*
oyster sauce, 49

pancakes
  Crispy Cheese Pancakes with
    Courgette Sauce, 32–3, *35*
paprika, 12, 34, 64, 82
Paradise Dessert, 97, *98*
Paradise Pork, *79*, 81
Parmesan cheese, 16, 32, 88
parsley, 17, 24, 25, 28, 43, 45, 53, 60,
  61, 62, 70, 73, 74, 86, 88
parsnips
  Savoury Parsnip Scones, 33, *35*
pasta
  Cheesy Spirals, *39*, 41
  Speedy Pasta, *87*, 88
pastry
  choux, 116–17
  filo, 20, 73
  puff, 89
  shortcrust, 61
Paté, Smooth Chicken, 14, *15*
Peach and Orange Sorbet, 112, *118*
peanuts, 34, 46
pears, dried, 128
Pears in Red Wine Syrup, *99*, 103
peas
  Petits Pois and Courgette Soup,
    27, 29
peppercorns, 14, 49
peppers
  Benedictine Curried Chicken, *50*, 53
  Chicken and Pork in Black Bean
    Sauce, 75, *78*
  Fakenham Fricassée, *87*, 92
  Huntsmans Loaf, 56, *59*
  Macaroni and Lentil Bake, *39*, 40
  Paradise Pork, *78*, 81
  Spicy Beef and Pepper Hot Pot,
    82, *83*
  Taylor Toad Supreme, 64, *67*
  Vegetable Curry, *42*, 46

Petits Pois and Courgette Soup, 27, 29
pine nuts, 32
pineapple
    Chicken Tropical, 77, 78
    Creamy Topped Carrot Cake, 134,
        137
    Pineapple Ice Cream in Ginger
        Baskets, 102–3, 107
pineapple juice, 81
pizza
    Savoury Pizzas, 37, 39
plaice, 73
poppy seeds, 127
pork
    Chicken and Pork in Black Bean
        Sauce, 75, 78
    Fillet of Pork Parcels with Apple
        Rings, 62, 63
    Garlic Chicken, 91, 93
    Paradise Pork, 78, 81
    Pork 'n' Cider, 67, 69
    Pork Thingies, 87, 88
    Pork with Beer Sauce, 65, 67
    Spicy Spare Ribs, 78, 80
    Stilton Stuffed Pork in Pastry, 83,
        89
    Taylor Toad Supreme, 64, 67
port, 56, 89
potatoes
    Aduki Bean Moussaka, 42, 44
    Cold Chive and Potato Soup with
        Cheese, 27, 28
    Leek and Roquefort Soup, 22, 26
    Mrs M's Mussel Soup, 24, 26
    1930 Carrot Pudding, 110, 111
    Salmon Fish Cakes, 70, 71
    Savoury Pizzas, 37, 39
    Tandoori Chicken with Green
        Bananas, 50, 52
    Tangy Vegetable Au Gratin, 38, 39
prawns
    Blushing Smoked Trout Mousse,
        12, 15
    Flaky Fish Surprise, 71, 73
    Prawn and Brie Strudels, 18, 20
    Seafood Lasagne, 71, 72
Profiteroles with Banana Cream, 116–
    17, 119
puff pastry, 89

Rabbit Casserole, 59, 60
Raisin Loaf, 133, 134
raisins, 48, 61, 111, 113, 116, 133,
    140
raspberry liqueur, 120
raspberries
    Caramelised Raspberry Dessert,
        118, 120
    Elizabeth's Raspberry Duck, 55, 57
    Hazelnut and Raspberry
        Meringue, 98, 101
redcurrant jelly, 62
rice, 53, 69
Rich Fruit Cake, 126, 140
Ricotta cheese, 32
Roquefort cheese, 22
rum, 111

saffron, 48
sage, 62, 69, 80
sage and onion stuffing, 34
salad
    Exotic Tofu with Melon Salad, 35,
        36
salmon
    Salmon Fish Cakes, 70, 71
    Salmon Mousse, 13, 15
    Salmon Surprise, 61, 63

sauce
    beer, 65
    black bean, 75
    brown, 77
    cheese, 38, 44
    courgette, 33
    herb and lemon, 61
    oyster, 49
    soy, 44, 75, 76, 80, 81, 93
    tomato, 45
    white, 40
    Worcester, 80, 82
sausagemeat, 62
sausages, 64
Savoury Artichoke Spread, 15, 16
Savoury Parsnip Scones, 33, 35
Savoury Pizzas, 37, 39
Scones, Savoury Parsnip, 33, 35
Seafood Lasagne, 71, 72
sesame oil, 88
sesame seeds, 41
Shahi Murghi (Royal Chicken), 48,
    51
shallots, 24, 32–3, 36, 49, 61
sherry, 14, 21, 77, 140
Shortbread, Marigold, 130, 131
shortcrust pastry, 61
Smooth Chicken Paté, 14, 15
soft cheese, 45
Sorbet, Peach and Orange, 112, 118
Soufflé, Mock Lobster, 18, 21
soups
    Carrot and Coriander Seed Soup,
        23, 26
    Cold Chive and Potato Soup with
        Cheese, 27, 28
    Leek and Roquefort Soup, 22, 26
    Mrs M's Mussel Soup, 24, 26
    Mushroom Bisque, 25, 27
    Petits Pois and Courgette Soup,
        27, 29
    Spinach and Cheese Soup, 27, 30
soy sauce, 44, 75, 76, 80, 81, 93
Spare Ribs, Spicy, 78, 80
Speedy Pasta, 87, 88
Spicy Beef and Pepper Hot Pot, 82,
    83
Spicy Coated Leg of Lamb, 51, 54
Spicy Spare Ribs, 78, 80
Spinach and Cheese Soup, 27, 30
sponge fingers, 121, 125
Steak with Fetta Salad, 86, 87
stewing steak, 82
Stewkey Sea Food Cobbler, 71, 74
Stilton cheese, 22
    Cold Chive and Potato Soup with
        Cheese, 27, 28
    Stilton Stuffed Pork in Pastry, 83,
        89
stock, 62
    beef, 58, 82
    chicken, 25, 28, 29, 30, 53, 57, 66,
        77, 92, 93
    fish, 12
    vegetable, 22, 23, 44, 46, 82
Strawberry Gateau, 125, 126
Stuffed Aubergines, 42, 45
suet, 111
sultanas
    Apple and Sultana Cake, 132, 134
    Autumn Bars, 128, 130
    Banana Bread, 135, 136
    Bread Pudding, 113, 114
    Chicken Tropical, 77, 78
    Country Apple Pud, 114, 116
    Golden Cake, 135, 139
    Rich Fruit Cake, 134, 140
    Vegetable Curry, 42, 46

sunflower oil, 29
sweetcorn, 81
Swiss Truffle Cake, 123, 126

tagliatelle, 85
Tandoori Chicken with Green
    Bananas, 50, 52
Tandoori paste, 52
Tangy Vegetable Au Gratin, 38, 39
tarragon
    Salmon Surprise, 61, 62
    Tarragon Lamb Bake, 67, 68
Taylor Toad Supreme, 64, 67
Tia Maria, 116–17
tofu
    Exotic Tofu with Melon Salad, 35,
        36
    Savoury Parsnip Scones, 33, 35
tomato purée, 21, 37, 44, 72, 76, 80,
    83, 84, 91
tomato sauce, 45
tomatoes, 13, 24, 38, 40, 44, 46, 56,
    66, 72, 82, 83, 86, 94
trifle sponges, 100
trout
    Blushing Smoked Trout Mousse,
        12, 15
turkey
    Fakenham Fricassée, 87, 92
    Turkey Loaf, 90, 91
turkey stock, 90
turmeric, 36, 46, 52, 53, 54

unsalted butter, 106, 111, 123, 128

vanilla essence, 101, 105, 108, 133, 137
vanilla sugar, 101
Veal, Medallions of, 55, 56
Vegetable Curry, 42, 46
vegetable oil, 65, 66, 75, 77, 80, 81,
    84, 90
vegetable stock, 22, 23, 44, 46, 82
Vegetarian Stuffed Marrow, 34, 35
Venison Carbonade, 58, 59
vermouth
    Garlic and Vermouth Mushrooms,
        17, 18
vinegar, 101
    cider, 81
    wine, 57, 58

walnuts, 121, 137
waterchestnuts, 53
watercress, 62
Whisky Ginger Cream, 98, 100
White Chocolate Mousse with
    Raspberry Coulis, 10, 107
white sauce, 40
wine
    dry white, 60, 74, 94
    Pears in Red Wine Syrup, 99, 103
    red, 40, 103, 138
    rosé, 12
    white, 24, 25, 53, 57, 93
wine vinegar, 57, 58
Worcester sauce, 80, 82

yoghurt
    Exotic Tofu with Melon Salad, 35,
        36
    Fresh Melon with Stem Ginger and
        Yoghurt, 18, 19
    Prawn and Brie Strudels, 18, 20
    Speedy Pasta, 87, 88
    Spicy Coated Leg of Lamb, 51, 54
    Tandoori Chicken with Green
        Bananas, 50, 52

Acknowledgments

There is a huge team of collaborators behind this book and they all need a special mention and personal thanks. First and most important of all are the readers of *Prima* who sent in their recipes, not simply the one hundred who won a place in this book but all those who took the time and trouble to send in their ideas – choosing just one hundred was very difficult! Next the cookery team at *Prima*, brilliantly organised by their editor Clare Gordon-Smith, who with photographer Martin Brigdale took on the huge task of testing, cooking and photographing the delicious recipes I am sure you cannot wait to try. Many thanks to Family Choice produced by Booker Cash & Carry who sponsored the competition and gave so much help, Hodder & Stoughton publishers who produced this book, Campbell & Associates who promoted the competition and Kodak who kindly donated the film for the photographs. A well deserved vote of thanks must also go to the panel of judges – Jane Asher, Sue James, Editor of *Prima*, Clare Gordon-Smith of *Prima* and Debra Argue of Booker Cash & Carry – who carefully read, selected and grouped the hundreds and hundreds of recipes that poured in from all over the country.

May I personally take this opportunity to thank you for supporting CHILD 2000 and wish you many hours of pleasure and satisfaction from this book.

Julia Lindley-French
Director, CHILD 2000

Jane Asher

Sue James

Clare Gordon-Smith

Debra Argue